The Book of Hierarchies

THE BOOK OF HIERARCHIES

A Compendium of Steps,
Ranks, Orders, Levels,
Classes, Grades, Tiers,
Arrays, Degrees, Lines,
Divisions, Categories,
Precedents, Priorities,
and Other Distinctions

Lisbeth Mark

WILLIAM MORROW AND COMPANY, INC.
New York ◆ 1984

Library of Congress Catalog Card Number: 83–63030

ISBN: 0–688–02208–1
ISBN: 0–688–02646–X (pbk)

Printed in the United States of America

First Edition

1 2 3 4 5 6 7 8 9 10

BOOK DESIGN BY ELLEN LO GIUDICE

For WALLACE HAMILTON,
a fine writer

◆◆◆◆◆◆◆◆◆◆◆◆◆◆◆◆◆◆◆◆◆◆◆◆◆◆◆◆◆◆◆◆◆◆◆◆◆◆◆

Acknowledgments

My love and gratitude to Barbara Binswanger, Jim Charlton, Lucianne Goldberg, Chuck Newman, and my editor extraordinaire, Nick Bakalar. You are my own private choir of angels.

Unqualified, unclassified, undivided, non-hierarchical thanks to my family, the Newmans, the Goldbergs, the Hoopers, the Singers, the Levys, Helene Hatcher, Jesse Wright, Patricia Roberts, John Wykert, Cynthia Critchell Hildebrand, Kemp Miles, Robin Landy, Greg Amadon, and my friends who rallied and encouraged me from start to finish. Special thanks to Nakula and Jessica for their superb suggestions.

Contents

◆◆◆

Introduction

How many times have you missed the subplot of a war movie because you didn't understand that the Duke outranked Robert Mitchum? How much of Charles and Diana's wedding went over your head because you couldn't tell a baronet from a marquis? How long did it take you to recognize Alexander Haig's gaff when he claimed control of the country?

It's a matter of understanding hierarchies. A hierarchy is any established order based upon value, status, priority, importance, rank, relativity, personal taste, and/or natural law. Hierarchies can be distinctly subjective (my dog is better than your dog) or universally constant (on a ship the captain gives the orders).

Hierarchies provide a system of incentives while establishing boundaries. We make the grade, move on to the next level, or claw our way up. The physical manifestation of a hierarchy is a pyramid with the supreme ruler at the top (Gladys Knight, for example) and the subordinates in descending classifications below (the Pips, the back-up singers, the band, etc.).

The word "hierarchy" comes from the Greek roots *hieros*, meaning sacred, and *archos*, meaning leader. *Hieraeches* is Greek for "high priest." The first definitions offered by dictionaries have to do with religious orders and ranks. The hierarchy of the Roman Catholic Church specifically symbolizes the higher order of heaven through the actual structure of the church members and the spiritual teachings. Hierarchies mirror natural law. Corporate structures are not unlike a hive of honeybees or an ant colony.

The inclination to form hierarchies goes beyond having British genes. We do it instinctively and cling to them religiously. We buy Grade "A" eggs, attend "B" movies, and settle for a "C" on our long overdue Taft-Hartley paper. To say you are too much of an egalitarian to be class-conscious can mean only one thing—you are royalty.

We are born our own universe. We are profoundly self-centered until we become aware of our dependence on Mummy for food. This is our first encounter of a hierarchical kind.

Hierarchies become more complex as we move through childhood and adolescence and become more social (or antisocial as the case may be). Your personal hierarchy has gone from:

me   to   me

mother   them

orthodontists

Priorities shift and change as our lives become an intricate series of these overlapping pyramids. We talk about chains of command, totem poles, ladders of success, class distinctions, and pecking orders (which, after all, are based on barnyard reality).

Social hierarchies have been with us since the dawn of time. Caste systems are still very much a part of life in India, Asia, Africa, and on Nantucket.

The American Revolution aside, we are a country fascinated by and devoted to hierarchies. Swift, Orwell, Huxley, and even Mother Goose satirized our preoccupation with status. Scarlett spurned Rhett because he was not a gentleman, as Cathy turned away from Heathcliffe who was not to the manner (or manor) born. Poor Eliza Doolittle struggled to please Professor Higgins by speaking, walking, dressing, and acting like a "lady." Everyone who could beg or borrow a television set sat riveted to *Upstairs, Downstairs* and *Brideshead Revisited,* the British imports. We giggle over *The Official Preppy Handbook* and buy any magazine with Prince William on the cover. Who are we kidding?

Colloquialisms and language epitomize how we think hierarchically. Cream is rich and forms on top of milk, and so we refer to the elite as the cream of the crop or the cream of society. Similarly, consider the following expressions: uppercrust, hobnob (which means, literally, to have or have not), refined (free from impurities), and classy (that is, having "it"). On the other side of the scale, words or expressions having to do with the lower gradations center around the physically earthbound: seedy, dregs, scum of the earth, or tinny.

This book is made up of examples of hierarchies I found appealing, amusing, and enlightening. There is no excuse now when Prince William Arthur Philip Louis gets married, not to know if his bride is a worthy match. Never be confused by another rerun of *M*A*S*H* when Captain Pierce is nearly court-martialed for being rude to a major. Does a flush really beat a full house? Who is next in line for the presidency if the secretary of transportation is incapacitated? Is my dog better than yours?

CHAPTER ONE

Choir of Angels

The word "hierarchy," as we noted in the introduction, literally means "sacred leader." It is no accident that the pyramids of the Middle East, South America, and Mexico are shaped the way they are. Like Gothic architecture, all the structures point dramatically heavenward. Symbolically, the laity should make the spiritual effort to be near their god. A massive spire or pyramid immediately reminds people where they stand in the great scheme of things.

In the hierarchy of the Roman Catholic Church, the angels rank just below God Himself (or Herself). Saint Hildegard wrote:

> God orders every man so that the lower estate shall not raise itself above the higher, as once did Satan and the first man . . . God divides his people on earth into different estates, just as His Angels in Heaven are divided in different groups, angels and archangels . . . cherubim and seraphim.

The hierarchy of angels is the most consistently used example of a hierarchy in the dictionary because it is a perfect manifestation—so to speak.

Angels outrank the apostles in the hierarchy of heaven. There are levels within the host of angels that indicate their degree of perfection, their nature, and their grace. These levels are called choirs.

In descending order, the hierarchy of angels is:

First Choir
Seraphim
Cherubim
Thrones

Second Choir
Dominations (or Dominions)
Virtues
Powers

Third Choir
Principalities
Archangels
Angels

Remember the film *It's a Wonderful Life*? Jimmy Stewart was rescued by his guardian angel after jumping into the icy river. The Catholic Church assures its members that each one

has a guardian angel of his own. They are chosen from the lower choir and if they save Jimmy Stewart, presumably they move up a notch.

Dante, in *The Divine Comedy*, delineated the levels of Paradise, Hell, and Purgatory according to the classifications of sins and based upon the writings of Aristotle and Cicero. Dante wrote of three types of sin: Incontinence, Violence, and Fraud (or Malice). He then subclassified these into seven circles of Hell: four of Incontinence, one of Violence, and two of Fraud.

These are categories of unethical behavior. Dante was a Christian and so added two circles of wrong belief: Unbelief (Limbo) and Mischief (Heresy). These make up the total of nine circles of Hell. To Vestibule of the Futile he assigned those who had no faith or good works to recommend them.

The Circle of Violence is subdivided into three Rings; the Circle of Fraud Simple into ten Bowges; and, the Circle of Fraud Complex into four Regions. Hell, then, has twenty-four sections, according to Dante.

Beneath the earth's surface:

Dark Forest
Gate of Hell

Vestibule
Acheron
Limbo
   Lustful
   Gluttonous
   Hoarders and Spendthrifts
   Wrathful (River Styx)

City of Dis—Heresy

Phlegethon—River of Fire
Wood of Suicides
The Abominable Sand

The Great Barrier and Waterfall
   Panderers and Seducers
   Flatterers
   Simoniacs
   Sorcerers
   Barrators
   Hypocrites
   Thieves
   Counselors of Fraud
   Sowers of Discord
   Falsifiers

The Well—the Giants

Cocytus
Traitors to Kindred, Country, Guests, and Lords

Earth's Center

Upper Hell encircled Acheron down through to the River Styx. Everything below is considered Nether Hell.

Purgatory was imagined as a mountain again divided

into seven Cornices whereon the seven Capital Sins were
purged.

Upper Purgatory
  Disordered Love of Good
    Cornice 7—Lustful
    Cornice 6—Gluttonous
    Cornice 5—Covetous

Middle Purgatory
    Cornice 4—Slothful

Lower Purgatory
  Love of Neighbor's Harm (Love Perverted)
    Cornice 3—Wrathful
    Cornice 2—Envious
    Cornice 1—Proud

Peter's Gate: 3 steps: 3—Satisfaction
                   2—Contrition
                   1—Confession

Ante-Purgatory (Those who died unprepared—after a period of
time, a sort of detention; they will eventually be admitted into
Purgatory to wash away their sins and ascend to Paradise)

  Terrace 2
    Indolent
    Unshriven
    Preoccupied

  Terrace 1
    the Excommunicate

Finally, Paradise was divided into seven heavens, a celestial
ladder, and then three more heavens.

First heaven: Moon—where Angels dwell
Second heaven: Mercury—Archangels
Third heaven: Venus—Principalities

Fourth heaven: Sun—Powers
Fifth heaven: Mars—Virtues
Sixth heaven: Jupiter—Dominations
Seventh heaven: Saturn—Thrones
Celestial Ladder
Eighth heaven: fixed stars—Cherubim
Ninth heaven: Primum Mobile—Seraphim
Tenth heaven: Empyrean

Dante wins my personal award for excellence in hierarchical thinking. And he wasn't even English.

The Catholic Church has sustained itself as an institution for an impressively long time and one could speculate that the rigidity of its hierarchical structure is in part responsible.

The pope is the supreme authority in Catholicism, with the cardinals in the second most important position. The pope is chosen by the cardinals but does not have to be a cardinal himself when selected.

The hierarchy, then, is as follows:

Pope	the supreme authority
Cardinal	a prince of the Catholic Church—there are three categories: 1. Cardinal Bishop (there are six living in Rome) 2. Cardinal Priest (usually Bishops or Archbishops) 3. Cardinal Deacons These three groups make up the College of Cardinals.
Archbishop	title given to a Bishop who governs one or more dioceses or districts
Bishop	head of a single diocese or district
Monsignor	an honorary title
Priest	usually has jurisdiction over a parish
Deacon	first of the major orders but lowest in the hierarchy

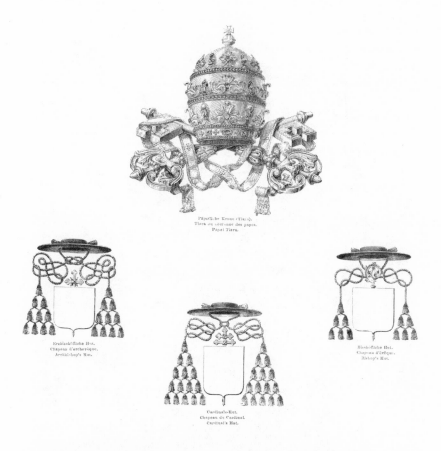

Päpstliche Krone (Tiara).
Tiare ou couronne des papes.
Papal Tiara.

Erzbischöfliche Hut.
Chapeau d'archevêque.
Archbishop's Hat.

Bischöfliche Hut.
Chapeau d'évêque.
Bishop's Hat.

Cardinals-Hut.
Chapeau de Cardinal.
Cardinal's Hat.

Abbots, guardians, priors, and rectors are titles given to the "superiors" of religious orders, such as the Jesuits or Franciscans.

In the past, initiates to a religious order had to go through several stages before taking final vows and becoming full members. A hopeful would have his "right stuff"* tested as he moved

---

*In his book about the history of the space program, *The Right Stuff*, Tom Wolfe explains the right stuff in terms of an ancient clan of South American Indians who tested their manhood by attempting to scale the treacherously jagged pyramids, called ziggurats, built as religious icons. To lose your footing or falter for a split second meant death. Men with the right stuff made it to the top of the pyramid—and down again.

up the ladder from postulant to novitiate. Obedience, poverty, and chastity were the three evangelical counsels of perfection.

As an example, those who aspired to join the Benedictines centuries ago had to be serious-minded (not just looking for free meals and an easy escape from the plague). The Rule of Saint Benedict was to test applicants' motives to see "whether they came from God." An applicant found himself knocking at the gates of the monastery for a very long time, and if he persevered for "four or five days . . . then let admittance be granted to him and let him stay at the guest house for a few days." One can only hope that he was also given ice for his swollen hand and a few days to rest up. The Benedictines must have had a peculiar sense of humor.

The Anglican Church was born out of the Reformation movement in England. They created a subtler hierarchy based upon the type of scriptures used and upon the relative closeness they maintained with the Catholic Church. The British (the true masters of hierarchical ways) divided the Anglican Church into:

Low Church—where scriptures were based upon the Reformation Church
High Church—where scriptures were interpreted in terms of the Catholic Church

The Ancient Greeks had a more simplified world view. Plato theorized that the universe (which then meant a limited radius around Athens) was a Great Chain of Being wherein all things (organic and inorganic) fell into a series of gradations arranged hierarchically below the gods, who sat at the summit of Olympus. The Great Chain of Being was layered this way:

Gods
Angels
Man
Animals
Plants
Rocks
(and other
inorganic
matter)

Whereas man was separated from the angels and the gods by his unfortunate tendency toward mortality, he was blessed with an intellect, which kept him a stone's throw above flora, fauna, and geologic *schmutz*.

The basic concept of the Great Chain of Being survived through to Elizabethan England. William Shakespeare celebrated man's special position in this hierarchy when he wrote this speech for Hamlet:

What a piece of work is a man! how noble in reason! how infinite in faculties! in form and moving how express and admirable! in action how like an angel! in apprehension how like a god! the beauty of the world! the paragon of animals!

Of course, Hamlet said this, then offed his uncle, drove Ophelia mad, and alienated half of Denmark with his unprincely behavior.

Eastern religions have a variety of hierarchical systems. Zen Buddhism, for example, is based upon a tenet that life is a continuous process of learning and seeking perfection. The irony is that Zen masters teach followers never to become preoccupied with or seduced by the desire to achieve the next level in the continuum. The emphasis is on meditation, training, and development of the inner qualities. The true student of Zen will reach divine freedom and knowledge without any conspicuous effort.

Zen teaches that there are six worlds (or *Lokas*) that stand for the states of mind produced by greed, hate, and delusion. Similar to the Great Chain of Being, the Lokas are classified:

Heaven
Humans
Animals
Asura
Hungry Ghosts
Hell

Lokas are classically drawn in a circular design with a snake (hate), a pig (greed), and a cock (delusion) chasing one another in the center. Lokas are states of mind that result from ignorance and materialism, as opposed to actual places one endures in life, or goes to in death.

In modern Western society, and on Sunday morning cartoons, a dilemma is often pictured as an angel whispering in one ear and a devil in the other. Dante described hell in very precise

hierarchical terms. If you didn't listen to the angel while on earth, the devil got you in the afterlife.

The flipside to the hierarchy of heaven is the kingdom of the devil. In the highly structured underworld where Lucifer reigns, there are scores of demons and no-good-niks who do his bidding. The grimoires are a sort of bible of demonology and the black arts. These ancient texts describe the hierarchy of hell. Keep in mind that this pecking order is a *descending* hierarchy; that is, the higher you rank in hell, the more evil you are. There is still some hope for redemption if your rank is low.

As there are several versions of the Bible, so there are different grimoires. The following is a more prevalent list of the most popular evil spirits. Every spirit has secret talents and special abilities that are carefully delineated in the grimoires. Heaven forbid you should send a lock specialist to hypnotize a cat!

In descending order (or ascending, depending on your point of view), the hierarchy of evil spirits is:

The Superior Spirits:
  Lucifer—Emperor
  Beelzebub—Prince
  Astaroth—Grand Duke

Each Superior Spirit has two inferiors who patrol the continents:

Lucifer: Satanchia, Agaliarept — Europe and Asia
Beelzebub: Tarchimache, Fleurety — Africa
Astaroth: Sargatanas, Nebrios — North and South America

Lucifuge Rofocale	—Prime Minister	most evil
Satanchia	—Commander-in-Chief	
Agaliarept	—Another Commander	
Fleurety	—Lieutenant General	
Sargatanas	—Brigadier General	
Nebrios	—Field Marshall and In-	least evil
	spector General	

Lucifuge Rofocale has control over wealth and treasures. Subordinates: Beel, Agares, Marbas

Satanchia has control over wives and maidens to do as he wishes. Subordinates: Pruslas, Aamon, Barbatos

Agaliarept has the faculty to discover arcane secrets in government and unveils most sublime mysteries. Commands the 2nd Legion of Spirits. Subordinates: Buer, Gusoyn, Botis

Fleurety has the power to perform any labor at night and can cause hailstorms. Controls a huge army of spirits. Subordinates: Bathsin, Pursan, Eligar

Sargatanas has the power to make anyone invisible, to transport him anywhere, to open all locks, to reveal whatever is taking place in private houses, to teach all the arts of shepherds. Commands several brigades of spirits. Subordinates: Zoray, Valefar, Faraii

Nebrios has the power to inflict evil on whomsoever he will; reveals every virtue of metals, minerals, vegetables, and animals; predicts future; is one of the greatest necromancers in the infernal hierarchies. Subordinates: Ayperos, Naberis, Glassyalabolas

CHAPTER TWO

High Societies

Historians have long been attracted to hierarchies as a way of explaining trends, upheavals, and downturns. The Greek poet Hesiod prophesied that mankind would go through five phases that had been foretold in mythology. Like the first biblical "fall," the states would begin with perfection and end in total decline.

Hesiod's hierarchy is as follows:

The Golden Age would be akin to the reign of the mythological king, Cronus. It would be a time of peace and prosperity.

The Silver Age would be a time when people would fall victim to their own pride, and sinning would become a popular pastime.

The Bronze Age would herald an age of violence. The discovery of the tools of war would give rise to chaos.

The Heroic Age might sound hopeful but would parallel the siege of Troy, and everyone would be reduced to fighting for their lives.

The Iron Age would see the final deathblow to civilization. Mankind would succumb to injustice, dishonesty, and greed, and would start to spell "civilization" with a "z" instead of an "s."

Remember the plaster of paris monstrosity you labored over in grade school? It was supposed to be a scale model of a feudal manor, but when your brother used the castle as a dartboard, even you questioned how many extra credit points it was really worth.

The feudal system in Europe was a hierarchy at work. The lord, who either inherited his land, won it in war, or received it as a gift from a grateful king, acted as overseer and protector

to his family and his serfs. The few skilled laborers of the time established guilds, which were mini–trade unions. There were three classes of free workmen (not free services—free as in not enslaved): the master craftsman, the apprentice, and the journeyman.

Before Commodore Perry stumbled onto the island, Japan

was an elaborately hierarchical feudal society and had remained virtually unchanged for centuries. The ruling class, the shoguns, created a self-perpetuating line and the emperor was revered as divine. Theoretically, no man or woman could rise above the class he or she was born into.

Japanese society was made up of four classes that were, in descending order:

Soldiers (Samurai)
Farmers
Artisans
Traders

There were gradations within each class and so there was some limited social movement. A gentry class evolved (as it eventually had in Europe) with the growth of urban centers, and was encouraged by long periods of peace. Artisans and craftspeople formed guilds and were afforded a new social respect depending upon the nature of their work. A swordsmith, for example, would be treated with special favors because of his value to a shogun.

Shoguns issued strict codes that were to be obeyed. These sumptuary laws were taken very seriously by everyone and helped to remind the peasant that the ruling class *was* different. For example, the Shogun Ieyasu dictated the following in 1615:

All costumes and ornaments are to be appropriate to the wearer's rank, and not extravagant in color or pattern. Common people are not to ride in palanquins without permission. Exception is made for physicians, astrologers, aged persons and invalids.

Sumptuary laws grew up in all sorts of societies all over the world. In England, for example, only a member of the royal family could hunt with a falcon (my ancestors used killer

geese). In Poland, a wealthy man could easily be spotted by the exaggerated curlicue at the toe of his shoes; the idea being that the rich need never have to run for anything.

Sumptuary laws kept the "haves" from mistakenly rubbing elbows (or curlicued slippers) with the "ain't gots."

The caste system of India is an example of sumptuary laws taken a few steps too far. It is based upon the Indians' belief in reincarnation. If a man lives a particularly good life, he will be rewarded in the next by, perhaps, moving up the scale. The "untouchables" are to be despised by everyone because they had obviously led a bad life the life before. Catch-22.

The Indian castes are as follows:

Brahman—the sacerdotal class (or priests)
Kshatriyas—the military class
Vaisyas—the mercantile class
Sudras—the servile class

The term "outcast" refers to being, literally, thrown out of one's caste.

There are seven words in Quechua, a South Amerind language, that refer to the hierarchical society of the Incans.

Curaco—Indian noble
Palla—Indian princess
Guaso—agricultural laborer
Yanacona—serf
Chino—a woman of mixed blood
Mitimae—member of a race conquered by Incans
Chuncho—an uncivilized jungle native

The Victorians were ruthlessly class-conscious because they feared that with the rise of the gentry, the new middle class, and the squirearchy, the gradations of social classes were (horrors!) blurring. Victorians resisted this by reinstituting the qualities of "good breeding" (detectable by the length of one's forehead, which is where the term "highbrow" comes from), proper manners, and *haute couture.*

The Victorians spent most of their time making sure that the sun never set on their empire. Professionally, men were classified as:

Gentlemen (meaning they didn't have to work)
Ranking Military
Professionals
Employers or Managers
"Junior" Professionals
Clerks

Retailers
Skilled Laborers
Semi-skilled Laborers
Unskilled Laborers
Soldiers or Sailors

The Royals were considered a nonclass—they simply *were*, as Queen Victoria proved year after year after year.

CHAPTER THREE

The Head That Wears the Crown

Two events of the recent past touched off serious interest in political hierarchies: the wedding of Prince Charles of Wales and Lady Diana Spencer (and the birth of their child, Prince William), and the attempted assassination of President Ronald Reagan.

On the occasion of the royal wedding, the Archbishop of Canterbury (who, incidentally, ranks seventh after the Queen in the royal order of precedence) said it was the stuff of fairy tales. It was a day of pure enchantment for the millions who watched the ceremony via satellite.

However, many of the subtleties of the guest list and the backstage drama were lost on the American audience. Was a duke more impressive than a marquis? Was Lord Spencer's daughter a good match for the Prince of Wales? How will Diana sign her checks now? Did Princess Anne wear that hat out of spite? And why wasn't *I* invited?

Then Prince William arrived the following June, becoming next in line for the throne after his father. Did the bells in the

church towers peal so joyfully for William, or was it the realization that Princess Anne was being edged out?

The royal family is a hierarchy. Lines of succession, orders of precedence, titles, knighthood, and the pecking order of the royal staff, are all examples.

Queen Elizabeth is the reigning monarch. Her full title is: "Her Majesty Elizabeth II, Alexandra Mary, by the Grace of God, of the United Kingdom of Great Britain and Northern Ireland and of Her other Realms and Territories, Queen, Head of the Commonwealth, Defender of the Faith, Sovereign of the British Orders of Knighthood." She must have to use a rubber stamp when she signs documents.

Prince Charles's full title has a romantic quality about it: "His Royal Highness Charles Philip Arthur George, Prince of Wales and Earl of Chester, Duke of Cornwall and of Rothesay, Earl of Carrick and Lord of Renfrew, Lord of the Isles and Great Steward of Scotland."

For the record, Prince William fans, the British line of succession is as follows:

HRH The Prince of Wales
HRH The Prince William of Wales
HRH The Prince Andrew
HRH The Prince Edward
HRH The Princess Anne
Peter Phillips
Zara Phillips

HRH The Princess Margaret
Viscount Linley
Lady Sarah Armstrong-Jones
HRH The Duke of Gloucester
The Earl of Ulster
Lady Davina Windsor
Lady Rose Windsor
The Duke of Kent
The Earl of St. Andrews
Lord Nicholas Windsor
Lady Helen Windsor
Lord Frederick Windsor
Lady Gabriella Windsor
Princess Alexandra
James Ogilvy
Marina Ogilvy
The Earl of Harewood
Viscount Lascelles
Alexander Lascelles
The Honorable James Lascelles
Rowan Lascelles
Sophia Lascelles
The Honorable Robert Lascelles
The Honorable Gerald Lascelles
Henry Lascelles
The Duke of Fife
The Earl of Macduff
Lady Alexandra Carnegie
HM King Olav of Norway
HRH Crown Prince Harald of Norway
HRH Prince Haakon Magnus of Norway
HRH Princess Martha Louise of Norway
Princess Ragnhild, Mrs. Lorentzen
Haakon Lorentzen
Ingeborg Lorentzen
Ragnhild Lorentzen
Princess Astrid, Mrs. Ferner

Alexander Ferner
Carl Christian Ferner
Cathrine Ferner
Benedicte Ferner
Elisabeth Ferner
HRH Princess Margarita of Roumania
HRH Princess Helen of Roumania
HRH Princess Irina of Roumania
HRH Princess Sophie of Roumania
HRH Princess Maria of Roumania
HRH Prince Tomislav of Yugoslavia
HRH Prince Nikola of Yugoslavia

The peerage of Great Britain refers to the body of the five degrees of nobility: duke, marquis, earl, viscount, and baron (in descending order). A peer of the realm is entitled to a seat in the House of Lords, a listing in *Burke's Peerage*, and, presumably, decent service at a London restaurant.

Dukes (and duchesses) are ranked just below members of the blood royal and are titled "The Most Noble." All peers (and peeresses) below the ducal rank are called Lord (or Lady) and are addressed "The Most Honorable" (if a marquis or marchioness) and "The Right Honorable" (if an earl, viscount, or baron).

Contrary to popular belief, a baronet is not a baby (or short) baron. Baronet is a hereditary honor passed on from father to son. Below baronets rank the various orders of knighthood, which are not hereditary. The orders are as follows, listed according to their order of precedence:

The Most Noble Order of the Garter. This order is conferred only upon royals and peers, with a few very rare exceptions. The letters "K.G." follow the name and title of the conferee. This order was founded by Edward III, circa 1348, and consists of the sovereign and twenty-five Knights Companions. It is, along with the Thistle, the personal gift of the sovereign. Just to give you an idea, the insignia is made up of the Garter, the Collar, the Star, the George, and the Less George. The Garter is worn below the left knee (Ladies of the Order wear it on the left arm between shoulder and elbow). The Collar is gold and consists of twenty-four linked red roses within a representation of the Garter; the Star is eight-pointed and made of chipped silver. The George is gold and the design shows Saint George slaying the dragon. It is suspended by a sash on the right hip. There are also the mantle, the hood, the surcoat, and the hat.

The Most Ancient and Most Noble Order of the Thistle. This order is exclusively for Scottish nobles.

The Most Illustrious Order of Saint Patrick. Obviously, this order is exclusively for Irish nobles.

The Most Honourable Order of the Bath. This is the first of the orders of knighthood which can be conferred upon a commoner. There are three classes to the order and members of the first two classes are knights in the technical sense.
1. Knights Grand Cross
2. Knights Commanders
3. Companions

The Most Exalted Order of the Star of India. The same three classes apply here with slight name changes.
1. Knights Grand Commanders
2. Knights Commanders
3. Companions

The Most Distinguished Order of Saint Michael and Saint George. Same three classes as for the Bath.

The Most Eminent Order of the Indian Empire. Same three classes as for the Star of India.

The Royal Victorian Order. There are five classes for men and five classes for women.
1. Knights Grand Cross
2. Knights Commanders
3. Commanders
4. Members 4th class
5. Members 5th class

for women:
1. Dames Grand Cross
2. Dames Commanders
3. Commanders
4. Members 4th class
5. Members 5th class

The Most Excellent Order of the British Empire (sounds like Valleyspeak to me). This is a newer order and is also open to men and women. There are five classes for each, very similar to the Victorian Order.

Knights Bachelor. This is the lowest order of knighthood. After Knights Bachelors have been presented to the Queen, the widows of knights follow and, on their heels, the honorary orders of knighthood that are usually granted to foreigners who have amused the sovereign in some way. You can be a member of more than one order, in which case you rank your initials (such as O.B.E. and K.C.M.G.) hierarchically according to the highest order. While the first two classes of each order are entitled (so to speak) to use "Sir" or "Dame," the third, fourth, and fifth classes are stuck with "Esquire" or plain old "Miss, Mrs., or Mr."

A knight's coat of arms identifies his family, affiliation, and position among his male siblings. Cadency marks were once used within the design of a heraldic coat of arms to indicate each son's ranking in the order of birth. There were marks for up to nine brothers. The first son used the "Label," which is part of Prince Charles's coat of arms. The Label looks like a section of Stonehenge. The list of marks is as follows:

First Son: Label (three-footed "M" shape)
Second Son: Crescent
Third Son: Mullet (a five-pointed star)
Fourth Son: Martlet (a footless bird—the idea being that a
    fourth son had no property upon which to land)
Fifth Son: Annulet (a solid ring)
Sixth Son: Fleur-de-lys
Seventh Son: Rose
Eighth Son: Cross Moline (a fluted cross)
Ninth Son: Octofoil (an eight-pointed star shape)

The ancient rules of Scotland's clans and territorial houses, and Ireland's Brehon Law of the succession of chieftains, are still recognized in those countries.

In Scotland, the chiefs of the clans and houses are known by their territorial names and are rarely called mister or esquire. This dates back to feudal customs where, for example, MacKenzie of Cavanagh took the name Cavanagh.

Few direct bloodlines from the ancient Brehon Law of Irish succession have survived through this century. The list is registered in the genealogical office at Dublin Castle. When one family cannot offer any proof of membership to a senior line, the next family on the list takes over the chieftainship. The following is the ancient Gaelic order according to the Irish law:

MacDermot Prince of Coolavin
MacGillycuddy of the Reeks
MacMurrough Kavanagh
O'Brien of Thomond
O'Callaghan
O'Conor Don
O'Donel of Tirconnell
O'Donoghue of the Glens
O'Donovan
O'Morchoe
O'Neill of Clandeboy
O'Sionnaigh (called the Fox since 1552)
O'Toole of Fer Tire
O'Grady of Kilballyowen
O'Kelly of Gallagh and Tycooly

Consanguinity, a term rarely used now except in estate cases, is defined as blood relationship, or descent from a common ancestor. Consanguinity tables were kept by the church in the Middle Ages to ensure that intermarriage, particularly among the nobility, did not conflict with biblical taboos. The fundamental rule was that a man and woman could not marry if they had a common ancestor during the seven previous generations.

Consanguinity charts are more than simple family trees. The following explains the breakdown of common ancestry:

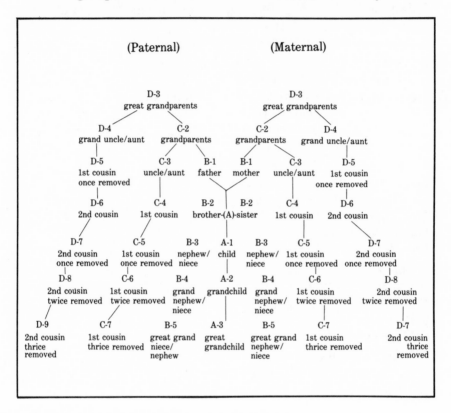

The letters B, C, and D identify the nearest ancestors in common with A. Numbers 1 through 9 indicate the degree of kinship to A under civil law.

The ancient Teutons developed a practice to keep ancestral lines "pure" and estates intact while still permitting a marriage based on love to take place. They invented the "morganatic marriage." This was so that a nobleman who wanted to marry a woman of a lower social rank could do so, but she would have no claim to his family name, title, arms, or property.

The marriage would be perfectly legitimate, as would the

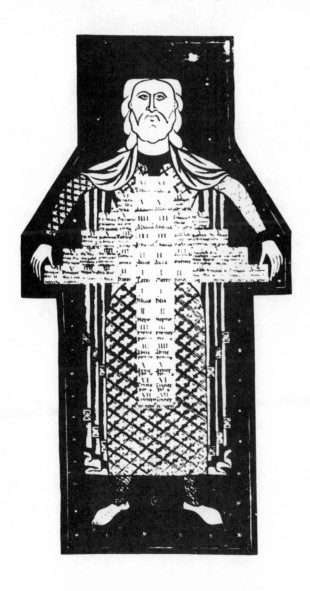

children, but wife and offspring would get nothing from the family. However, they stood to inherit what would be settled in a contract signed before the wedding ceremony took place. *Morgen-gave* is a German expression deriving from the tradition of the groom giving his bride a gift the morning after the day of the wedding.

When Queen Elizabeth's uncle gave up the throne of England for the woman he loved, it had been suggested that they investigate the possibility of a morganatic marriage so that he could still rule England. The suggestion obviously did not appeal to them.

After the fact, then Secretary of State Alexander Haig explained that he was winded from the jog to the press room and was cleverly letting the world know that someone was in fact in charge though the President was yukking it up with the nurses at George Washington University Hospital. Some students of political science wondered what had happened to the Vice President and the Speaker of the House.

If the President is incapacitated, the American line of succession does not permit Nancy, Ron Junior, Patti, or Maureen to step in. Or Al Haig. The chain of command is as follows:

President of the United States
Vice President
Speaker of the House of Representatives
President Pro Tempore of the Senate
Secretary of State
Secretary of the Treasury
Secretary of Defense
The Attorney General
Secretary of the Interior
Secretary of Agriculture
Secretary of Commerce
Secretary of Labor
Secretary of Health and Human Services
Secretary of Housing and Urban Development
Secretary of Transportation
Secretary of Energy
Secretary of Education

If the White House is nuked and the Secretary of Education survives, the New World will be founded upon the strength of our SAT scores.

CHAPTER FOUR

Not-So-Secret Societies

Driving through Small Town, U.S.A., you can't help noticing those low-slung brick buildings with life-sized plastic elk or moose on the lawn. The town's welcome sign is compliments of the Lions. The playground scoreboard is decorated with crests from the Rotarians, the Hibernians, and the Knights of Columbus. Who, you ask yourself, are these people, and why are they so enamored of large, furry animals?

These are the social and professional fraternities (and sororities) that grew up in this country in the latter part of the nineteenth century. Before trade unions, insurance, and Club Med, the average working man had no opportunity to protect himself from a financial disaster and to socialize with like-minded people. There was prejudice and social snobbery, and if *they* didn't want you in their town, you got packing. The secret societies (some of which had roots in Europe) provided benefits for the widows and orphans of members, and offered some social life and assurance that, at the end of the day, there would be a cozy spot to meet friends.

Though most of these organizations were socially oriented, some became and have remained politically powerful. The Molly Maguires, for example, were an offshoot of the ancient Hibernians of Ireland.

The Freemasons are probably the best known of the secret societies and provided the framework for most of the societies that were established in the United States. The Freemasons claim to be descendants of the builders (masons) of Solomon's Temple. Actually, they were founded at a London pub called the Goose and Gridiron in 1717 (A.D.!). They were a drinking society that developed into a trade union when the master masons of London didn't feel that their guilds were representing them effectively.

Freemasons base their founding principles upon the ancient craft of masonry and interpret their symbols and mythology in quasi-religious terms.

Many kings and United States presidents were Freemasons (including George Washington and Andrew Jackson). To get a feel for the influence the Freemasons had on this country, take a dollar bill from your wallet. The Great Seal of the United States is a Freemason design. The eagle is holding thirty-two feathers—and there are thirty-two degrees within the Scottish Rite of Masonry. The thirteen stars over the eagle's head form a Star of David, who had dreamed of building a temple. *E Pluribus Unum* is a motto of the Freemasons. Note the pyramid and the all-seeing eye—very Freemasonesque.

Rudyard Kipling wrote a thrilling adventure story titled *The*

Man Who Would Be King, based upon the lives of two adventurers whose association with Freemasonry made one of them king.

To become a member of the Freemasons, you must be willing to go through the secret rites of induction, and learn the insignia, handshakes, and passwords (without your Captain America decoder ring). If you repeat any of the secrets of the order, you should know that you will be buried up to your neck at low tide. This could be especially unpleasant if you live in New York City.

Upon induction into a lodge, one must achieve three degrees:

Entered Apprentice
Fellow Craft
Master Mason

If the competition appeals to you and you have paid the initiation fees, you work toward the 4th degree and up the ladder to the 32nd. Each degree has its own insignia, historical basis, and responsibilities to the office.

The 29 degrees from the 4th through the 32nd are grouped according to the Scottish Rite into the following categories:

Lodge of Perfection   4–14
Chapter Rose Croix   15–18
Council of Kadosh   19–30
Consistory   31–32

The following is the list of the different degrees available if you are willing to go the distance:

4th Secret Master
5th Perfect Master
6th Intimate Secretary
7th Provost and Judge
8th Intendent of the Building
9th Master Elect of Nine

10th Master Elect of Fifteen
11th Sublime Knight Elect
12th Grand Master Architect
13th Knight of the 9th Arch
14th Grand Elect Perfect and Sublime Mason
15th Knights of the East or Sword
16th Prince of Jerusalem
17th Knight of the East and West
18th Knight of the Rose Croix
19th Pontiff or Grand Pontiff
20th Master of the Symbolic Lodge or Master Ad Vitam
21st Noachite or Prussian Knight
22nd Knight of the Royal Axe or Prince of Libanus
23rd Chief of the Tabernacle
24th Prince of the Tabernacle
25th Knight of the Brazen Serpent
26th Prince of Mercy
27th Knight Commander of the Temple
28th Knight of the Sun or Prince Adept
29th Knight of Saint Andrew
30th Knight of Kadosh
31st Grand Inspector Inquisitor Commander
32nd Sublime Prince of the Royal Secret

I wonder if either Ralph or Norton ever made Sovereign Grand Inspector General of the Raccoons.

◆◆◆◆◆◆◆◆◆◆◆◆◆◆◆◆◆◆◆◆◆◆◆◆◆◆◆◆◆◆◆◆◆◆◆◆◆

CHAPTER FIVE

Now That's an Order

There is no organization in the United States or any other country more hierarchical than the military. It is defined by its systems of ranks, orders, and pay scale. As in secret societies, the military enjoys the use of badges, salutes, handshakes, uniforms, decorations, medals, and codes; they help to distinguish soldier from sailor, grunt from sergeant, a platoon from a squad, and, blessedly, John Wayne from Robert Mitchum.

The United States military is, of course, under the supreme command of the president of the United States.

The ranking of the members of the United States Army is as follows (the identifying insignia are included so you can see who is who when watching parades or war films):

Rank	Insignia
General of the Army	5 silver stars fastened in a circle with the coat of arms of the U.S. in the center
General	4 silver stars
Lieutenant General	3 silver stars
Major General	2 silver stars
Brigadier General	1 silver star
Colonel	silver eagle
Lieutenant Colonel	silver oak leaf
Major	gold oak leaf
Captain	2 silver bars
1st Lieutenant	1 silver bar
2nd Lieutenant	1 gold bar
(Noncoms)	
Sergeant Major of the Army	same as Command Sergeant Major but with 2 stars plus red and white shield on lapel
Command Sergeant Major	3 chevrons above 3 arcs with 5-pointed star with wreath around it in the center
Sergeant Major	3 chevrons above 3 arcs with 5-pointed star in the center
1st Sergeant	3 chevrons above 3 arcs with lozenge in the center
Master Sergeant	3 chevrons above 3 arcs
Platoon Sergeant (or Sergeant 1st Class)	3 chevrons above 2 arcs
Staff Sergeant	3 chevrons above 1 arc

Rank	Insignia
Sergeant	3 chevrons
Corporal	2 chevrons
(Specialists)	
Specialist 7	3 arcs above eagle device
Specialist 6	2 arcs above eagle device
Specialist 5	1 arc above eagle device
Specialist 4	eagle device only
(Other Enlisted Personel)	
Private 1st Class	1 chevron
Private (E-2)	none
Private (E-1)	none
Warrant Officers	
Grade 4	silver bar with 4 enamel black bands
Grade 3	silver bar with 3 enamel black bands
Grade 2	silver bar with 2 enamel black bands
Grade 1	silver bar with 1 enamel black band

The following Navy rank corresponds to the list of Army rank. If you are going to have an admiral or general as the hero in your next romantic war epic, strut your stuff and make him (or her) a fleet admiral or a brigadier general.

U.S. Navy Rank	Stripes/Stars	U.S. Army Rank
Fleet Admiral	5	General of the Army
Admiral	4	General
Vice-Admiral	3	Lieutenant General
Rear Admiral	2	Major General
Commodore	1	Brigadier General

The Navy ranks, after the rank of Commodore, are as follows:

Commissioned Officers
Captain
Commander
Lieutenant Commander
Lieutenant
Lieutenant Junior Grade
Ensign

Warrant Officers
Commissioned Warrant 4th grade
Commissioned Warrant 3rd grade

Commissioned Warrant 2nd grade
Warrant Officer 1st grade

Enlisted Personnel
Master Chief Petty Officer
Senior Chief Petty Officer
Chief Petty Officer
Petty Officer 1st Class
Petty Officer 2nd Class
Petty Officer 3rd Class
Seaman
Seaman Apprentice
Seaman Recruit

The pay scale corresponds to rank and to cumulative years of service. If, for example, you somehow manage to remain a seaman for over twenty-six years, you will get $732.90 per month. An admiral with over twenty-six years of service will receive $6,333.90 per month. So it's not just the chicness of the stripes that creates incentive. And rank certainly does have its privileges.

At the video game arcade you overhear the delighted shouts that your kid just wiped out a platoon of aliens. Is this good? Is it better than zapping, say, a brigade or a squadron? Check the list and react accordingly.

Army Units

Squad	in infantry, usually 10 men under a staff sargeant
Platoon	in infantry, 4 squads under a lieutenant
Company	HQ section and 4 platoons under a captain. In artillery it equals a battery and in the cavalry, a troop.
Battalion	HQ section and 4 or more companies under a lieutenant colonel. In cavalry it equals a squadron.
Brigade	HQ and 3 or more battalions under a colonel

Division	HQ and 3 brigades with artillery, combat support and combat service support units under a major general
Army Corps	2 or more divisions with corps troops under a lieutenant general
Field Army	HQ and 2 or more corps with field army troops under a general

Air Force Units
Flight
Squadron
Group
Wing
Air Division
Numbered Air Force
Major Command

It's not just John Wayne. There is the added problem of Basil Rathbone, Errol Flynn, and David Niven. Is a "leftenant" superior to a squadron leader? Is that why Errol never forgave Basil in *The Dawn Patrol*?

The British military rankings are, not surprisingly, very similar to those of the United States. However, when World War II got heated up and the United States became involved, we needed "brass" that would outrank their brass. So the Pentagon came up with four- and five-star generals. Five stars are rare in United States military history. Ulysses S. Grant was a three-star general and George Washington only managed one (but both were awarded their five stars posthumously).

The following is a comparative study of the ranks of officers in Her Majesty's Fighting Forces:

Royal Navy
Admiral of the Fleet
Admiral
Vice-Admiral

Rear Admiral
Commodore
Captain
Commander
Lieutenant Commander
Lieutenant
Sublieutenant
Midshipman (Lapel)

Army and Royal Marines
Field Marshal
General
Lieutenant General
Major General
Brigadier
Colonel
Lieutenant Colonel
Major
Captain
Lieutenant
Second Lieutenant

Royal Air Force
Marshal of the R.A.F.
Air Chief Marshal
Air Marshal
Air Vice-Marshal
Air Commodore
Group Captain
Wing Commander
Squadron Leader
Flight Lieutenant
Flying Officer (a neat trick)
Pilot Officer

Chains of command have been around since before the Roman Legions, before the Crusades, before the Force and the

Empire. It is impossible to imagine an army in the future where rank isn't used. The Starship *Enterprise* employed the following chain of command, folding in elements from the Army, the Navy, and Walter Reed Medical Center:

Captain—James T. Kirk
First Officer/Commander (and science expert)—Mr. Spock
Doctor and Lieutenant Commander—Leonard McCoy ("Bones")
Chief Engineer and Lieutenant Commander—Montgomery Scott ("Scottie")
Helmsman and Lieutenant—Sulu
Communications Lieutenant—Uhuru

Navigator Ensign—Pavel Chekov
Nurse—Christine Chapel

Anyone else introduced at the beginning of an episode stood a solid chance of being either lost in the beaming-up process or zapped by aliens. Only these regulars managed to survive from one star date to the next.

CHAPTER SIX

Making the Grades

Grade school, when you think about it, is remarkably aptly named. School provides us with our first serious encounters with hierarchies. As we move from one grade to the next, we gather points, stars, grades, and marks that, we are told, will go on our record for LIFE.

But even before we toddle off to preschool, we learn the basics at home. The Swiss psychologist Jean Piaget specialized in child development. He suggested that the first period of mental development begins at birth and continues through to the first sign of language. He called this the sensorimotor period.

birth–6 weeks	Development of reflexes
6 weeks–4 or 5 months	Development of habits
4–9 months	Coordination between vision and prehension
9–12 months	Coordination between means and goals
12–18 months	Discovery of new means
18–24 months	Insights

We are taught the hierarchies of things in nature and society when we are children. Games, songs, nursery rhymes, and fairy tales give us practical lessons on order. The ranking of family members, for example, is described in the circle game "The Farmer in the Dell." The farmer takes a wife and the wife takes a child. The child takes a dog that takes a cat that takes a rat that takes the cheese. The cheese stands alone. The game predates modern refrigeration.

"King of the Mountain" was a popular game with my brother and sisters when my parents went out to dinner. As soon as the car had pulled out of the driveway, we would denude the sofa of pillows and build the mountain. There would then be a mad scramble to exhaust everyone else and be the only one left atop the mountain while chanting, "I'm the king of the castle and you're the dirty rascal." By the end of the game the bulldog, Duncan, would sit like Jabba the Hutt—the unmovable beast— victorious atop the pillows. This game pointedly taught us the principle of survival of the fittest.

Nursery rhymes echo hierarchical orders. For example, "Lavender Blue" goes:

Lavender's blue, diddle, diddle,
Lavender's green.
When I am king, diddle, diddle,
You will be queen.

Call up your men, diddle, diddle,
Set them to work.
Some to the plough, diddle, diddle,
Some to the cart.

Some to make hay, diddle, diddle,
Some to cut corn,
While you and I, diddle, diddle,
Keep ourselves warm.

The little poem "To Mystery Land" carries a strong message about keeping one's place:

> Oh, dear, how will it end?
> Peggy and Susie how naughty you are.
> You little know where you are,
> Going so far, and so high,
> Nearly up to the sky.
> Perhaps it's a giant who lives there,
> And perhaps it's a lovely princess.
> But you will never know
> You have no business to go;
> You'll get yourselves into a mess.
> Oh, dear, I'm sure it's true;
> Whatever on earth can it matter to you?
> For you know it—oh fie—
> That it's naughty to pry
> Into other's affairs—
> Into other folks' houses to go,
> Where you know
> You are not asked.

So you'd better come back
While there is time, it's plain.
Go home—and never be so naughty again.

The Christmas song "The Twelve Days of Christmas" shows how extravagant gift giving was handled in days of yore:

A partridge in a pear tree
Two turtle doves
Three French hens
Four calling birds
Five golden rings
Six geese a-laying
Seven swans a-swimming
Eight maids a-milking
Nine ladies dancing
Ten lords a-leaping
Eleven pipers piping
Twelve drummers drumming

Imagine finding ten leaping lords beneath your tree on the tenth day of Christmas. "Oh, honey! You shouldn't have!"

As students in college, we are awarded degrees and honors and, if all goes well, a red Corvette. Graduating with honors is a very special thing. It's even more enjoyable if you understand what the Latin means:

Cum Laude: with praise
Magna Cum Laude: with great praise
Summa Cum Laude: with the greatest praise

James Lipton, in his exquisite book titled *An Exaltation of Larks*, collects all of those elusive terms that describe a grouping of something. His mini-hierarchy of academe is:

A plentitude of freshmen
A platitude of sophomores
A gratitude of juniors

An attitude of seniors
A fortitude of graduate students
An avunculus of alumni
A tenure of associate professors
An entrenchment of full professors

   Ivy League colleges, along with a few other like-minded institutions, rank their prospective freshmen on a five-to-one basis for both academic achievements and non-academic activities. While a non-academic "1" may have gotten his or her rating by writing a computer program or running a two-hour marathon (or even starring in *The Blue Lagoon*), an academic "1" is usually a combination of grades, teacher recommendations, and SAT and Board scores. A "1/1" at Yale or Princeton is a rare and highly prized applicant, and he or she is chased after the

way Notre Dame goes after tight ends or U.S.C. goes after cheerleaders.

The Scholastic Aptitude Test (SAT) is administered by the Educational Testing Service of Princeton, New Jersey. Roughly, one million college-bound seniors take this test each year and it is a requirement at virtually every college in the country. While SAT score averages have been consistently sliding downhill over the past twenty years, the percentages of students who tested for the 1981–82 academic year ranked as follows:

These figures are for the 1,040,550 college-bound seniors who took the test.

Educational Testing Service		
	Verbal	Math
750–800	less than 1%	1%
700–749	1%	2%
650–699	2%	4%
600–649	4%	8%
550–599	7%	12%
500–549	12%	13%
450–499	16%	15%
400–449	18%	15%
350–399	16%	13%
300–349	12%	10%
250–299	8%	5%
200–249	5%	1%
Average	426	467

CHAPTER SEVEN

Googols and Barrels

The sciences assign arbitrary numbers to things so that the unscientific and nonscientific among us can understand the basics.

Starting with the basics one of the first things a child learns is numbers. Numbers are what frame hierarchies to give them meaning.

Sadly, I was absent the day my class was taught Roman numerals. To this day I have trouble with crossword puzzles, cornerstones, and Tiffany watches. Until I actually memorize them, herewith the list for the other kids who had the mumps that day:

I   = One
V   = Five
X   = Ten
L   = Fifty
C   = One Hundred
D   = Five Hundred
M   = One Thousand

A dash over the letter (numeral) multiplies it by one thousand —a little bonus which no doubt developed after the fall of the Roman Empire because no one could think past one thousand. Wouldn't Caesar get a kick out of googols?

Googols? Googol (a name chosen by the nephew of mathematician Edward Kasner) is a word for the number one followed by a hundred zeros (equal to 10^{100}). A googolplex is a one followed by a googol of zeros (equal to $10^{10^{100}}$). (The mere thought cripples me with math anxiety.)

Remember when, as a kid, you were driving cross-country with your family? Remember starting to sing "One Trillion Bottles of Beer on the Wall" and that weird scream that came from your mother as she began banging her head against the dashboard of the car? Impress the math freaks in your life by memorizing the following "illions" chart:

Zeros	Illions
6	Million
9	Billion
12	Trillion
15	Quadrillion
18	Quintillion
21	Sextillion
24	Septillion
27	Octillion
30	Nonillion
33	Decillion
36	Undecillion
39	Duodecillion
42	Tredecillion
45	Quattuordecillion
48	Quindecillion
51	Sexdecillion
54	Septendecillion
57	Octodecillion
60	Novemdecillion
63	Vigintillion

The next thing you graduate to are polygons. I do have vague memories of learning the prefixes for them and I do know that a STOP sign is red and is something more than square. Better to have this list handy:

Shape	Sides
Triangle	3
Quadrilateral	4
Pentagon	5
Hexagon	6
Heptagon	7
Octagon	8
Nonagon	9
Decagon	10
Dodecagon	12

(Spirograph needed to continue)

Though the ranking of multiple births is fun for the grandparents, the mother and father of a group of new babies might feel differently. The odds on multiple births are as follows:

Twins	one out of every 80–100 births
Triplets	one out of every 10,000 births
Quadruplets	one out of every 600,000 births
Quintuplets	one out of every 85 million births
Sextuplets	too many zeros to think about
Septuplets	ibid
Octuplets	one out of a googol

The odds are based upon Hellin's Law and are calculated as follows: triplets number is arrived at by squaring the twinning rate, quads by cubing the twinning rate, quints by quadding the twinning rate, and so on. Makes meiosis look like a barrel of fun.

So the babies have arrived, all at once. It might be worthwhile to send baby announcements to everyone you've ever met and any relative you've ever had an address for. Add in this subtle little chart to help your friends abroad when they go looking for baby gifts:

Children
Dresses, Coats, Suits, Skirts, Pants—Junior Misses

United States	2	4	6	8	10	13	15
Great Britain	2	4	6	8	10	13	15
Europe	1	2	5	7	9	10	12

Most Apparel—Girls and Boys

United States	3	4	5	6	6X
Great Britain	18	20	22	24	26
Europe	98	104	110	116	122

Shoes—Girls and Boys

United States	8	9	10	11	12	13	1	2	3	4½
Great Britain	7	8	9	10	11	12	13	1	2	3
Europe	24	25	27	28	29	30	32	33	34	36

Please Note: Glove sizes are standard in the United States, Great Britain, and Continental Europe.

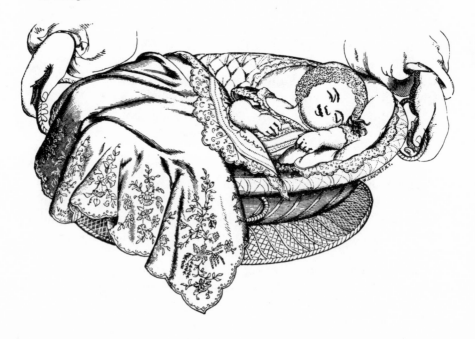

You are no doubt still reeling at the thought that the American dollar bill is covered with the symbols of Freemasons. United States coins, though, are pleasantly all-American and all sport presidents, with one notable exception (if we skip over coins minted before 1972).

Coins
.01 — Lincoln
.05 — Jefferson
.10 — Franklin D. Roosevelt
.25 — Washington
.50 — John F. Kennedy
1.00 — Eisenhower (or) Susan B. Anthony

Bills
$1 — Washington
 2 — Jefferson
 5 — Lincoln
10 — Hamilton
20 — Jackson
50 — Grant
100 — Franklin
500 — McKinley
1,000 — Cleveland
5,000 — Madison
10,000 — Salmon Chase

Now, without looking in your wallet, do you know who is on the 100,000-dollar bill? Give up? Okay, go ahead and look. Do you believe it? Woodie Wilson!

United States savings bonds are unique in that Teddy Roosevelt makes an appearance:

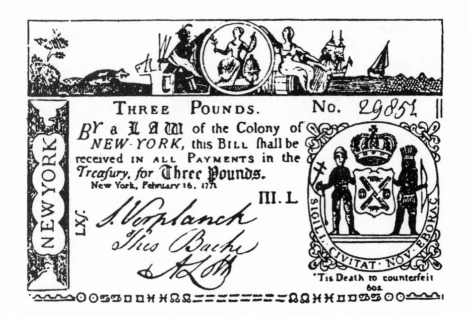

$25—Washington
 50—Jefferson
 75—John F. Kennedy
 100—Cleveland
 200—Franklin D. Roosevelt
 500—Wilson
 1,000—Lincoln
 10,000—Teddy Roosevelt

Money being the root of many hierarchies, it is a critical issue when interviewing for a job. Government positions are given a GS (General Schedule) rating. "Fred's landed a GS-14" sounds more refined than "Fred pulls down forty thou."

The salaries shown are based on the standard federal work week of forty hours. Additional pay is provided for authorized overtime and all basic salaries are subject to a deduction of 7 percent for retirement purposes.

The following is the General Schedule for entrance salaries for most white-collar government jobs (effective October 1982).

Salaries will differ slightly depending upon the type of job, the skills required, and the locale of the job itself.

Grade	Annual Salary
GS-1	$ 8,676
GS-2	9,756
GS-3	10,645
GS-4	11,949
GS-5	13,369
GS-6	14,901
GS-7	16,559
GS-8	18,339
GS-9	20,256
GS-10	22,307
GS-11	24,508
GS-12	29,374
GS-13	34,930
GS-14	41,277
GS-15	48,553

The hierarchy of gifts one gives upon a certain anniversary is interesting. It would appear, from the following list, that divorces and separations have been around since the dawn of Hallmark. Hold off on giving crystal or china until the couple proves their marriage will last beyond fifteen years. The first few anniversaries, though, make for interesting and kinky gift ideas.

 1 Cotton
 2 Paper
 3 Leather
 4 Flowers
 5 Wood
 6 Candy
 7 Wool/Copper
 8 Pottery/Bronze
 9 Willow/Wicker
10 Tin

11	Steel
12	Silk/Linen
13	Lace
14	Ivory
15	Crystal
20	China
25	Silver
30	Pearl
35	Coral
40	Ruby
45	Sapphire
50	Gold
55	Emerald
60	Diamond
70	Platinum

Picture it. You've been married two years. He comes home holding a daintily wrapped box. Jewelry? You happily undo the package as he watches. "Honey! How did you guess? My own packet of three-by-five index cards!" You can barely contain your joy as you melt into his arms.

You just had to sit through your best friend's boasting about her second anniversary gift. You decide it's time to accept your boyfriend's proposal and get married. You go ring shopping only to discover that you are totally ignorant about gold, karats, weights, purity, stones, gems, cuts, and settings. The trick is that most precious metals and stones are ranked and rated on hierarchical scales.

Consider gold, which has always been a symbol of superiority. You have a golden opportunity to take home the gold which is, after all, good as gold. Gold is classified by its purity, weight, and color.

The rating of 24K (karat) is given to "pure" gold, according to American standards. Being too soft to be made into lasting jewelry, it is alloyed (or mixed) with at least two of the following metals: copper, zinc, nickel, or silver. This alloying process strengthens the gold.

The number of karats indicates the ratio of gold to these alloyed metals. The ratings of 18K, 14K, and 10K are the most common karat numbers that you will see stamped onto jewelry. Ten is the lowest number of karats that can be sold in this country and still be considered gold.

Rose, white, yellow, or green gold refers to the type of alloy metal used in the mixing process.* However, the ratio of gold to metal doesn't change.

Lower content items are usually made by one of two processes: mechanical bonding or electroplating. These are the various techniques:

Gold-filled (also known as gold overlay): A layer of karat gold (meaning at least 10K) is mechanically bonded to a base metal. The karat gold must be at least $\frac{1}{20}$ of the total metal weight

*Rose gold is an alloy of gold with copper; white gold is an alloy of gold with platinum, palladium, and nickel; green gold is an alloy of gold with silver.

of the piece. The karat content of the gold will be marked, for example, as 14K G.F.

Rolled Gold-plate: The same technique as gold-filled but can be made with a thinner layer of gold. This is most often used in watches and the marking will indicate the amount of gold. For example, $\frac{1}{40}$ 14K R.G.P.

Heavy Gold Electroplate: A layer of karat gold is placed on a base metal. This has the thickest outer layer of gold of the electroplates and is the most durable.

Gold Electroplate: Same as above except the layer of gold is thinner (minimum requirement is 7-millionths of an inch).

Vermeil: Heavy gold electroplate over sterling silver.

Gold Wash (or Gold Flash): Also an electroplating process, but with a coating of gold thinner than required for gold electroplate.

One of the reasons gold has been universally sought after and revered is because of its workability. All metals are rated according to their malleability (the ability of the metal to be hammered or rolled into sheets or foil) and their ductility (how well the metal can be drawn into wire). These qualities are determined by the toughness and the strengths of the metals.

The following scale was developed by Charles H. Fulton to rank the workability of metals from easiest to most resistant:

Malleability	Ductility
Gold	Gold
Silver	Silver
Copper	Platinum
Platinum	Iron
Palladium	Nickel
Iron	Copper
Aluminum	Palladium
Tin	Aluminum

Zinc	Zinc
Lead	Tin
Nickel	Lead

Similar to Fulton's scale, Friedrich Mohs developed a scale for testing the strength and hardness of minerals. Diamond can scratch corundum (sapphire, for example), but not the other way around. It's an ideal method for testing the relative hardness of minerals in the field. Talc, obviously, is the softest. The following is Mohs' scale:

1) Talc
2) Gypsum
3) Calcite
4) Fluorite
5) Apatite
6) Feldspar
7) Quartz

8) Topaz
9) Corundum
10) Diamond

While most of us have been dragged reluctantly toward the age of metrics and the language of computers, it is comforting to know that our system of weights and measures has been around since man discovered that his thumb joint equaled, miraculously, one inch. The word "inch" derives from the Latin *uncia*, meaning the twelfth part. This proves that the foot came before the inch.

A hairbreadth measures .0208th of an inch—unless you are Farrah Fawcett. A barleycorn was an ancient measure that equaled ⅓ of an inch and is the basis, still, for determining a person's shoe size (on a scale of 13).

The four units based upon the measurement of a hand are:

Nail: equals 2¼ inches and is the length from the thumb-nail to the joint at the base of the thumb. This was once used for measuring fabrics.

Palm: equals 3 inches and is the breadth of the hand minus the thumb.

Hand: equals 4 inches and is the breadth of the palm. The hand is used in measuring the height of horses.

Finger: equals 3½ inches and is the length of the middle finger. Do not confuse this with the width of a finger, which is used for measuring shots of liquor and, some time ago, charges of powder for muskets.

Here is an interesting, if odd, assortment of measurements arranged from the shortest to the longest:

Pace: a convenient measure that equals an average stride, or about a yard. The military pace "double time" equals a cadence of 3 steps per second, while "quick time" equals 2 steps in a shorter stride of approximately 30 inches. Precise.

Fathom: an Anglo-Saxon word "faethm" means embrace. It is
    the length of rope between 2 hands when arms are out-
    stretched and is most often employed as a nautical term for
    the depth of water.

Bolt: a roll of cloth of approximately 40 yards, depending upon
    the manufacturer and the type of fabric.

Skein: this varies with the type of yarn, but usually measures
    120 yards.

Furlong: this used to mean, literally, the length of a furrow or
    the distance oxen could plow without having to rest. Now
    it means 220 yards.

Hank: is the length of a spool of yarn or thread and varies with
    the type of material. In cotton, a hank usually measures
    840 yards.

Nautical Mile: equals $\frac{1}{60}$th of the length of a degree of a great
    circle of the earth. This is not a perfect measure because
    the earth is not a perfect sphere. It equals approximately
    6,080.20 feet and should not be confused with a knot, which
    is a measure of speed. A knot is equal to 1 nautical mile per
    hour.

League: equals 3 miles on land and 3 nautical miles at sea.

Light-year: this is the distance light travels in 1 year (about 5.878 trillion miles).

The measures "bushel" and "barrel" were never standardized because of the problem of heaping, and a barrel of apples in Vermont was not necessarily the same make of barrel you'd find in upstate New York. At one time, every state had its own definition of a bushel and a barrel. Now a bushel equals four pecks and a barrel equals approximately thirty-one and a half gallons.

Coomb: equals 4 bushels
Firkin: equals ¼ of a barrel
Hogshead: equals 2 barrels
Pipe: equals 4 barrels
Tun: equals 8 barrels

Once the finite objects had been parceled off into neat, tidy hierarchies, man looked toward the infinite—space. Time to roll out the Latin prefixes and suffixes and assign names to these terrestrial and celestial layers.

Geologists divided the Earth into three zones:

Lithosphere: all solids from the Earth's surface to the Earth's center
Hydrosphere: all surface water
Atmosphere: the multi-layered gaseous envelope that surrounds the Earth's surface

They then divided the planet Earth into the following sections, innermost to outermost:

	Miles Below the Surface
Inner Core	3200–3958
Outer Core	1800–3200
Lower Mantle	560–1800
Upper Mantle	9–560
Crust, Lithosphere	0–9

The inner core is composed of molten gases and mineral gunk. Or maybe it's China, I forget which.

Then, meteorologists named the layers beyond the atmosphere so folk like Chuck Yeager, John Glenn, and Sally Ride would know where they were at all times.

Troposphere
Stratosphere
Mesosphere
Thermosphere
Ionosphere
Exosphere

Never tell a geologist how good the sand feels between your toes as you meander along the shoreline. The romantic mood will inevitably be shattered when he or she corrects you by explaining that you are actually digging your toes into silt because of the average grain size.

Texture	Grain size (mm.)
Granule, Pebble, Cobble	2 or larger
Sand-size grain	0.0625–2
Silt-size grain	0.0039–0.0625
Clay-size grain	less than 0.0039

Similarly, don't tell a geologist you have something the size of a boulder under your contact lens. The thought may cause queasiness when you understand why.

Fragment	Diameter (mm.)
Boulder	more than 256
Cobble	64–256
Pebble	4–64
Granule	2–4

Sir Francis Beaufort (a scientist *and* an Englishman, which makes him twice as susceptible to hierarchical influences) de-

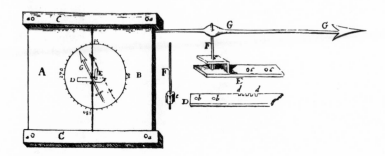

Beaufort Number	MPH	Knots	International Description	Specifications
0	less than 1	less than 1	Calm	Calm; smoke rises vertically.
1	1–3	1–3	Light air	Direction of wind shows by smoke drift but not by wind vanes.
2	4–7	4–6	Light breeze	Wind felt on face; leaves rustle; vanes moved by wind.
3	8–12	7–10	Gentle breeze	Leaves and small twigs in constant motion; wind extends light flag.
4	13–18	11–16	Moderate	Raises dust, loose paper; small branches move.
5	19–24	17–21	Fresh	Small trees begin to sway; crested wavelets form on inland water.
6	25–31	22–27	Strong	Large branches in motion; umbrella used with difficulty.

Beaufort Number	MPH	Knots	International Description	Specifications
7	32–38	28–33	Near gale	Whole trees in motion; inconvenience felt walking against wind.
8	39–46	34–40	Gale	Breaks twigs off trees; impedes progress.
9	47–54	41–47	Strong gale	Slight structural damage occurs.
10	55–63	48–55	Storm	Trees uprooted; considerable damage occurs.
11	64–72	56–63	Violent storm	Widespread damage.
12	73–82	64–71	Hurricane	Devastation.

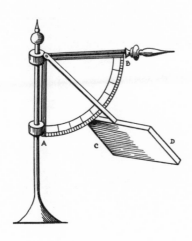

vised a scale to measure the strength of the wind. In 1805 he drew up what is known, aptly, as the Beaufort scale, and it is still in use when modern instruments are unavailable (having been blown into the next county). Some hairsetting gels resist number twelve on the Beaufort scale.

If *The Wizard of Oz* was rewritten and set in present-day California, the story might be about a hazardous PSI situation wherein Dorothy (the ultimate Valley girl) is knocked out by grody air quality and comes to in Montana thanks to the quick-thinking local surfers.

PSI stands for Pollutant Standard Index and was developed by the South Coast Air Quality Management District of El Monte, California, and the Environmental Protection Agency.

The numbers represent the density levels of ozone in parts per million. Five hundred PSI is awesome and could do more than gag you with a spoon.

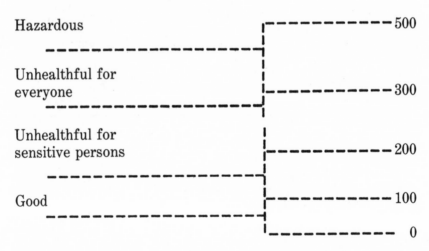

Hazardous — 500

Unhealthful for everyone — 300

Unhealthful for sensitive persons — 200

Good — 100

0

Beaufort's isn't the only scale that has survived the passage of time. Mercalli's intensity scale is still used for measuring earthquakes when the seismographs (upon which the Gutenberg-Richter scale of 1–10 is based) have been trashed. The Mercalli scale is based upon the description of the quake as opposed to an actual measurement.

When the San Andreas Fault of California finally does swallow up that state, scientists from the rest of the world may have to piece together the final minutes of the life of Los Angeles from survivors claiming it was tubular.

The Mercalli scale is as follows:

1. Detectable by experienced observers when lying down
2. Detectable by a few; delicately poised objects may move
3. There is some vibration; still unnoticed by many
4. Felt by many indoors; some moderate vibrations
5. Felt by almost everyone; unstable objects will move
6. Felt by everyone; strong vibrations and heavy objects will move
7. Very strong vibrations; weak buildings damaged
8. General damage in all but quake-proof buildings; objects overturned
9. Buildings shifted from foundations; collapse; some ground cracks
10. Serious ground fissures; larger buildings damaged or destroyed
11. Few if any structures will survive—catastrophic
12. Total devastation; vibrations strong enough to distort vision

Weathermen have a hierarchical language that seems suspiciously cryptic. What do they mean when they say moderate to heavy precipitation? Is it time for a raincoat or will an umbrella suffice? The United States Weather Bureau has explained it all for us by describing exactly what weatherese means:

Intensity of Precipitation (other than drizzle) on Rate-of-Fall Basis:

Very Light: scattered drops or flakes that do not completely wet or cover an exposed surface, regardless of duration

Light: trace to 0.10 inch per hour; maximum 0.01 inch in six minutes

Moderate: 0.11 inch to 0.30 inch per hour; more than 0.01 inch to 0.03 inch in six minutes

Heavy: more than 0.30 inch per hour; more than 0.03 inch in six minutes

Intensity of Drizzle on Rate-of-Fall Basis:
Very Light: scattered drops that do not completely wet an exposed surface, regardless of duration

Light: trace to 0.01 inch per hour

Moderate: more than 0.01 inch to 0.02 inch per hour

Heavy: more than 0.02 inch per hour

Intensity of Drizzle and Snow with Visibility as Criterion
Very Light: scattered flakes or droplets that do not completely cover or wet an exposed surface, regardless of duration

Light: visibility of ⅝ statute mile or more

Moderate: visibility less than ⅝ statute mile but more than $5/16$ statute mile

Heavy: visibility less than $5/16$ statute mile

Those weatherpeople can also be a bit vague about such things as "scattered sun" or "slight gusts." Does a "slight gust" mean I'll be walking knock-kneed to keep my dress from wrapping itself around my head? These meteorological vagaries do have very specific definitions.

Sky Cover Classifications

Clear:	cloudless or sky cover is less than 0.1
Scattered:	0.1–0.5 at and below the level of a layer aloft
Broken:	0.6–0.9 at and below the level of a layer aloft
Overcast:	1.0 at and below the level of a layer aloft
Partly Obscured:	1.0 or more but not all of the sky is hidden by surface-based obscuring phenomenon
Obscured:	sky is completely hidden by surface-based obscuring phenomenon (such as smoke or fog)

"Wind" is defined by the U.S. Weather Bureau as "horizontal motion of the air past a given point." Then things pick up speed:

Light Wind: speed is 6 knots or less
Gust: sudden surge in wind speed to more than 16 knots with a variation of 9 knots or more between peak and lull
Squall: sudden surge in wind by at least 16 knots and rising to 32 knots or more and lasting for at least one minute
Wind Shift: change in wind direction of 45 degrees or more that takes place in less than 15 minutes

You are contemplating spending the day on a friend's boat and so you listen to the nautical weather report on the radio. The announcer tells you the sea is "phenomenal." Great! You hop into your car and drive three hours to the marina only to find your friend mourning the tiny splinters floating in the slip. The forty-five-foot waves made kindling out of his boat. What happened? Phenomenal, in sea parlance, is a bit different from the way Howard Cosell used the word on Super Bowl Sunday.

Code Figure	Description of Sea	Maximum Height of Waves in Feet
0	calm–glassy	0
1	calm–rippled	0–1
2	smooth–wavelets	1–2
3	slight	2–4
4	moderate	4–8
5	rough	8–13
6	very rough	13–20
7	high	20–30
8	very high	30–45
9	phenomenal	45 and over

Why didn't the threatening clouds make a bigger impression on you before you made the three-hour trip to the U.S.S. *Matchstick*? Clouds, too, are named hierarchically.

The following is a list of clouds from, with some overlapping, the highest to the lowest:

Type of Cloud	Height in Feet
Cirrus	16,500–45,000
Cirrocumulus	1,500–6,500
Cirrostratus	16,500–45,000
Altocumulus	16,500–45,000
Cumulus	6,500–23,000
Stratocumulus	surface to 1,500
Cumulonimbus	1,500–6,500
Stratus	1,500–6,500

So the boat is ruined. That's no reason for your tan to suffer. Just remember that suntan lotion is always a good idea—no matter how swarthy or sun sensitive you are. Choose a brand that has an SPF number so you know exactly how much protection you are getting. SPF stands for:

SUN PROTECTION FACTOR.

When containers of suntan lotion, cream, oil, or gel have a number printed on them, it refers to the number of times it increases your natural protection from the sun. The scale is as follows:

Skin Type*	Protection Needed	Suggested SPF to Develop Base Tan
Rarely burns, tans easily (dark complexion)	Minimal	2
Burns minimally, tans well (normal skin)	Moderate	4

*Descriptions of the skin types are a matter of record in the *Federal Register*, August 1978.

| Burns moderately, tans gradually | Extra | 6 |
| Always burns easily, never tans (fair skin) | Maximal | 8 |

SPF's are available in 2, 4, 6, 8, and 15. Fifteen is a total sun block.

Moving along the Great Chain of Being from the inorganic to the organic, to which we, with a few exceptions, belong, Carl Linnaeus (a Swedish botanist and biologist) introduced the biological classifications in 1758. Linnaeus wanted to establish a system whereby different types of flora and fauna could be rated according to their complexity, and his system is still in use.

Kingdom
  subkingdom

Phylum/Division
  subphylum/subdivision
  superclass

Class
  subclass
  infraclass
  cohort
  superorder

Order
  suborder
  superfamily

Family
  subfamily
  tribe
  genus
  subgenus

Species
  subspecies

For an example of the power and innateness of hierarchies in nature, take a close (but not too close) look at a beehive or an ant colony. Shakespeare wrote,

> . . . for so work the honey bees,
> Creatures that by a rule in nature teach
> The act of order to a peopled kingdom.
> (*Henry V*, Act I, scene ii)

Honeybees are a society and, as such, are divided according to their physical makeup, their sex, and their occupations. Sounds strangely familiar, doesn't it?

The beehive is divided into:

Queen Bee
Drones
Workers

The bees are rigidly hierarchical. There is only one queen per honeybee colony. She doesn't exactly "rule" the roost, but she is revered and catered to as the mother of all the eggs in the hive. She's a busy, well, uh, bee, and so isn't expected to do much hivework.

Any bee can become queen (sounds like a game show, doesn't it?) and, once selected, she is attended to from egghood by her worker bees.

Worker bees are exclusively female and can do anything except reproduce. Only the queen has that capacity. Young workers clean hive until they are ready to take short flights out into the world. Some will remain as guards, while others begin a life of foraging.

Drones are always male. They have superior vision and wing strength, which are employed to propel them to the queen to reproduce. Once they have performed this, their only function, they are killed. So much for responsible parenting and teaching the little beelets how to play ball.

Ants are as class-conscious as bees. They are divided into:

Queen
Worker
Soldiers:
    Giants—super soldiers
    Pygmies—little soldiers

As in a beehive, every ant colony has a mother queen. Workers are the queen's daughters who are either infertile or less fertile than their mother. Their duty is to collect food (tuna

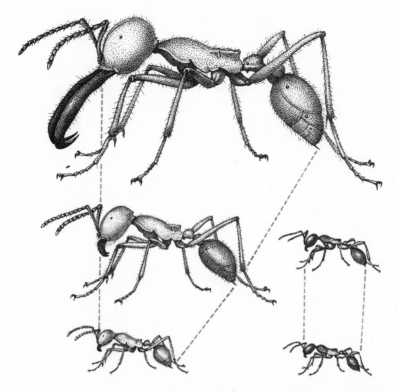

sandwiches, hot dog rolls, deviled eggs, and Oreos are popular) and to feed the queen and the larvae.

The soldiers are a special category of workers and are also female. Physically they have larger heads that they use to block entrances to the colony when threatened. They principally defend the home and are also excellent diggers.

Giant soldiers (and the larger workers) tend to be more aggressive and adventurous. Pygmy soldiers and the smaller workers stay close to the colony.

Ants move along through three stages of physical development before they are recognizable as those little varmints we see on sidewalks and at picnics. They start off as eggs, become larvae, and, eventually, pupae.

Most animal groups do cling to a hierarchical family structure. Elephants, wolves, whales, dolphins, and swans are profoundly dedicated to their families and to the larger group. The family can be a source of strength or angst.

Two decades ago Doctor Holmes and his colleagues at the University of Washington in Seattle developed the Social Readjustment Rating Scale. This hierarchy of stressful situations is based upon their decision to rate getting married at an arbitrary fifty points. Then, comparing marriage to other events, catastrophes and happy occasions, they devised the following scale:

Death of a spouse	100 points
Divorce	73
Marital separation	65
Jail term	63
Death of a close family member	63
Personal injury or illness	53
Marriage	50
Being fired	47
Marital reconciliation	45
Retirement	45
Pregnancy	40
Gaining a new family member	39
Death of a close friend	36
Changing careers	35
Major change in job description	29
In-law problems	29
Outstanding personal victory	28
Starting or ending formal schooling	26
Trouble with your boss	23
Major change in social activities	18
Vacation	13
Christmas	12

Enjoying some kind of personal best, then, can be as stressful as having a run-in with your boss. If several of these situations occur at once, you may want to consider seeking professional help.

Americans have always worshiped their automobiles. They name them Imperial, LeBaron, Marquis, and Grand Prix. The Environmental Protection Agency and the Department of Energy put their collective heads together and came up with the following definitions for the size of the car. This will come in very handy the next time you call to rent a car and don't know what the reservationist means when he or she asks if you want a subcompact.

Two Seater

Sedan:

Minicompact:	less than 85 cubic feet of passenger and luggage volume
Subcompact:	85–100 cubic feet of passenger and luggage volume
Compact:	100–110 cubic feet
Mid-Size:	110–120 cubic feet
Large:	120 or more cubic feet

Station Wagon:

Small:	less than 130 cubic feet of passenger and cargo volume
Mid-Size:	130–160 cubic feet
Large:	160 or more cubic feet

Truck:

Small: having Gross Vehicle Weight Rating under 4,500 pounds

Standard: having G.V.W.R. between 4,500 and 8,500 pounds

You cannot haul cargo in a sedan—only in a station wagon. Remember that.

I have never been a terrific driver. I am, however, an excellent passenger—provided I get the front seat by the window. The following hierarchy of desirability of seating in a car is acknowledged by siblings universally:

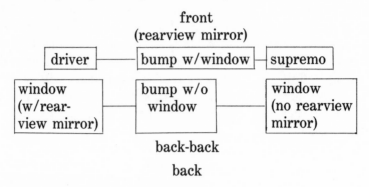

front
(rearview mirror)

driver	bump w/window	supremo
window (w/rear-view mirror)	bump w/o window	window (no rearview mirror)

back-back

back

Ranked according to desirability:
1—Front seat by the window
2—Window and no rearview mirror
3—Window but in direct line of driver's rearview mirror
4—Bump but a wide window and access to radio
5—Bump, no window and someone on either side—no foot room
6—Slow death (back-back)

While on the subject of travel, consider the word "posh" (meaning "super luxurious" or "ultra elegant"). It is thought to be an acronym for "port out, starboard home." When Britannia ruled the waves, English families traveled by ship to far-flung tropical colonies. The most desirable cabins were located portside on the way out and starboard on the way back —out of the direct heat of the sun.

CHAPTER EIGHT

Class Acts

The world of show business provides its own microcosm of hierarchies from the so-called star system, to top billing and the order of credits in a film. Actors talk in terms of "leads" and secondary roles. Critics rate films on a 1–10 scale, and some give stars, the same way restaurant critics rate restaurants. Films are sometimes rated as "B" movies and are distributed differently from the first-rate features.

One of the oldest traditions of the theater has to do with the subtle priorities accorded the stars. One such tradition is the position, size, and accessibility of the star's dressing room. The dressing rooms at the Metropolitan Opera House at New York's Lincoln Center, for example, are arranged thus:

Women	*Men*
S20 S22 S24	S30 S32 S34
S18	S36
S16 S14 S12 S10	S8 S6 S4 S2

stage

The position of the dressing room reflects the importance of the role of the singer. The level of one's position in the show decides how close one will be to the stage. The room S8 is reserved for the male star and S10 for the female star.

The audience should not feel left out of the pecking order and traditions of the theater. The next time you attend the theater, ballet, or a concert, flip through the program to the section explaining the trustee system. Also note that those who choose to donate money to the theater are ranked according to how much they give.

The New York Philharmonic tempts you by assigning the name "sustaining contributor" if you part with $10,000:

Sustaining Contributor	$10,000
Guarantor	5,000
Sponsor	2,500
Patron	1,200
Donor	500

However, the system differs from one theater to the next. A patron, therefore, is not always a sponsor. The Manhattan Theater Club is more sympathetic and understands that most theatergoers have trashed their savings to afford shows. Their system is:

Supporter	under $50
Patron	$50–149
Associate	150–499
Donor	500–1,249
Benefactor	1,250–2,499
Angel	2,500–4,999
Pacesetter	5,000–9,999
Sustainer	10,000 or more

Most of us know the fundamentals of the musical scale, thanks to Julie Andrews. Musical notes, though, are more com-

plicated. They do form a perfect little triangle and serve the purposes of this book very handily.

The score for a country and western song may lean heavily on the whole notes while "Flight of the Bumble Bee" in notation looks like a computer printout.

To really impress your date at a concert, during intermission suggest that the conductor was too heavy on the "adagio"— that the piece requires "pianissimo." But first, make sure he or she did not compose the piece. For a full listing:

Grave	solemn (very slow)
Largo	broad (very slow)
Adagio	quite slow
Lento	slow

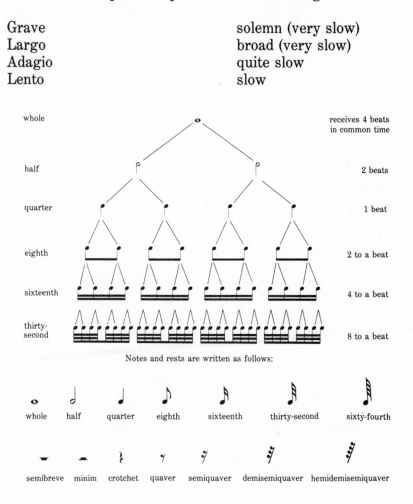

Notes and rests are written as follows:

CLASS ACTS ◆ 105

Andante	a walking pace
Andantino	somewhat faster than andante
Moderato	moderate
Allegretto	moderately fast
Allegro	fast (cheerful)
Vivace	lively
Presto	very fast
Prestissimo	very very fast
	Modifying Adverbs
Molto	very
Meno	less
Poco	a little
Non Troppo	not too much
	Tempo Change
Accelerando	getting faster
Ritardando	holding back /getting slower
A Tempo	in time
	Dynamics/Musical Volume
Pianissimo (pp)	very soft
Piano (p)	soft
Mezzo Piano (mp)	moderately soft
Mezzo Forte (mf)	moderately loud
Forte (f)	loud
Fortissimo (ff)	very loud
	Change in Dynamics
Crescendo	growing louder
Decrescendo or Diminuendo	growing softer

One of the biggest shocks in my career as a member of the Gordon Junior High School Glee Club (the sign in the hall said "Tryouts: No One Turned Down") was being asked to lip-sync at the Dogwood Festival. I longed to be a fair-haired soprano

but the crushing reality was that I was a tenor. A tone-deaf
tenor.

The following explains the range of the human voice in terms
of the classifications:

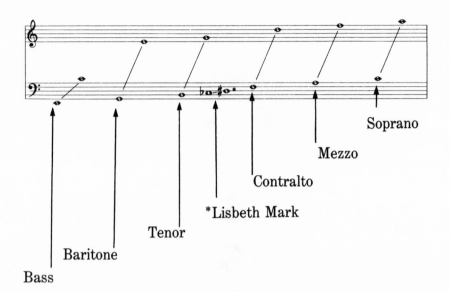

Soprano

Mezzo

Contralto

*Lisbeth Mark

Tenor

Baritone

Bass

Vocal range does not always a great singer make. The following list explains how the diadem of country music stars is broken down:

Jimmie Rodgers — Father of country music
Maybelle Carter — Mother of country music
Roy Acuff — King of country music
Kitty Wells — Queen of country music
Tammy Wynette — First Lady of country music
Conway Twitty — High Priest of country music
George Jones — Crown Prince of country music
Joe and Rose Lee Maphis — Mr. and Mrs. Country Music

But Elvis will always be The King.

CHAPTER NINE

Cream of the Crop

The world of food lends itself naturally to ranks, orders, and classifications. A chef strives for the *Cordon Bleu* degree; a new restaurant works desperately hard for a multi-star rating; the United States Department of Agriculture inspects food and grades it with indelible purple ink.

The USDA rates meat according to the quality, value, cut, and grade. Most cuts of beef, veal, calf, lamb, yearling mutton, and mutton will have a ribbon-like stamp on it that tells you the quality grade mark. From the highest quality to the lowest, they are graded:

USDA Prime
USDA Choice
USDA Good
USDA Standard (STNDRD)
USDA Commercial (COMRCL)
USDA Utility

Interestingly, the USDA recently reworked their beef-grading system and instead of getting high marks for marbled, fattier beef, you now get the higher marks for leaner cuts.

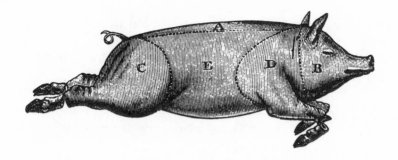

Eggs are graded and sized and sold in supermarkets if they are Medium size and weight or heavier. Pullets, plovers, and pigeons now only make rare appearances on educational TV specials about the life of Evelyn Waugh. This is how they are sized:

1 dozen Extra Large eggs must weigh at least 27 ounces.
1 dozen Large eggs must weigh at least 24 ounces.
1 dozen Medium eggs must weigh at least 21 ounces.

They are graded according to their yolk/white ratio. The eggs must be of a specific physical size to qualify for each category. Six Extra Large and 6 Medium *do not* equal 1 dozen Large eggs.

Grade AA eggs are general purpose with thick whites and firm yolks that are virtually free from defects.

Grade A eggs are also general purpose but may have a defect or two.
Grade B eggs are not usually sold at retail but are usable for general cooking and baking.

The USDA also grades the quality level of fruits and vegetables. They agree that taste is, well, a matter of taste.

U.S. Grade A means excellent color and flavor, uniformity of shape and size, few defects—use when appearance is most important.
U.S. Grade B means good quality and suitable for most purposes.
U.S. Grade C guarantees you value when appearance is not crucial and you just want to make your point at a political rally.

The California Olive Growers have published guidelines for rating those tasty little morsels:

Classification	Whole Pitted or Unpitted
Small	128–140 per pound
Medium	106–121 per pound
Large	91–105 per pound
Extra Large	65–88 per pound
Jumbo	51–60 per pound
Colossal	41–50 per pound
Super Colossal	26–40 per pound
Leviathan	1 per pound, and it ate New York City in *The Attack of the Killer Pimentos*

Symbols are often used to denote the quality of a product—like the star system on brandies, for example. The "x" symbol, it is believed, dates back to early Christianity. Shortly after the death of Christ, bakers and millers started marking sacks of flour with three xs as a reminder of the three crosses of Calvary. Later, superior flour was marked with the three xs.

Charles A. Pillsbury thought his flour was the best on the market and so adopted the trademark that incorporates four xs.

The "x" was also a symbol used by distilleries to show how many times a liquor had been distilled. The symbol XXXX stood for the strongest and the purest. Later it came to mean, simply, that the beer or liquor was of a certain strength. It is no longer used except in cartoons of Saint Bernards, with tiny kegs of brandy strapped to their collars, rescuing skiers.

The "V.S.O." marking on a bottle of cognac tells the buyer the quality and age of the liquor:

V.S.O.   =very special old
V.S.O.P.   =very special old pale
V.V.S.O.P.   =very very special old pale

Champagne is often used as a modifying adjective because it has long been a symbol of indulgence. Although the larger bottles are hard to find these days, champagne is still the Rolls-Royce of wines.

Split   187 ml.
Half bottle   375 ml.
Bottle   750 ml.
Magnum   1.5 liters (2 bottles)
Jeroboam   3 liters (4 bottles)

After a Jeroboam, champagne may legally be bottled in an even liter size above three liters:

Rehoboam (no longer a legal size)   4.5 liters or 6 bottles
Methuselah   6 liters or 8 bottles
Salmanazar   9 liters or 12 bottles

| Balthazar | 12 liters or 16 bottles |
| Nebuchadnezzar | 15 liters or 20 bottles |

Ordering champagne is a nice gesture, but to really impress your dinner partners, drop the following pearls: Jeroboam was the first king of Israel and Rehoboam was the king who eventually defeated him. Methuselah was a 969-year-old patriarch. Balthazar was a Babylonian king and Nebuchadnezzar was his grandfather. Salmanazar was an Abyssinian warrior king.

The French, wine connoisseurs that they are, were the first to attempt to rank wine. They limited themselves at first to the Médoc region (an area that stretches northwesterly along the Gironde River) where most of the great red wines are produced. Many attempts were made at classifying wines, and in 1855, the awards were made. Four châteaux were given first place, fifteen second, fourteen third, ten fourth and seventeen fifth. Some changes have taken place, but the ranks still stand today. Château Mouton-Rothschild, arguably one of the most enjoyable wines in the world, was classified in the second *cru*, but has since moved into the top rank.

French vintners have tried to restructure the system, but, in the final analysis, the old classifications remain the same. The *premiers crus* are:

Lafite
Latour
Margaux
Châteaux Mouton-Rothschild
Haut-Brion Graves

Wine is not the only food to be graded according to vintage. Olive oil, vinegars, and maple syrups are graded and ascribed a vintage.

Vermont maple syrup has a heavier density than the average

syrup. According to the Mandatory Maple Syrup Grading Law of Vermont, syrups are rated:

Fancy (vintage): light amber color and a delicate bouquet distinguish this grade.
Grade A: medium amber color with a more pronounced maple flavor. This is the one you soak your pancakes and French toast in.
Grade B: dark amber color with a heavier flavor and a slight, sweet caramel taste. This type is used more for cooking and flavoring.
Grade C: dark amber color with a heavy caramel flavor. Strongest maple flavor of all four grades, this type is used in making candies and in cooking.

Food critics rate restaurants according to their own codes of excellence. The *Guide Michelin* gives stars from the point of view of the traveler; that is, is it worth going out of your way for a particular eatery?

Being considered the cream of the crop by the big cheese is no small potatoes.

―

CHAPTER TEN

Win, Place, and Show

Gold, silver, and bronze medals; first, second, and third place; blue, red, and white ribbons; win, place, and show. From your first egg and spoon race on, you are taught the value of winning. To the victor go the spoils, the gold, the blue ribbon, the "return."

Some sports and games are based upon ancient hierarchies. Take a close look at a chess board. Placed according to their strength and maneuverability are kings, queens, knights, bishops, castles (rooks), and pawns. (Pretty well sums up the structure in your office, right?)

Games are based upon the incentive system. This is the motivating force behind functional hierarchies.

Consider the historical significance of a deck of cards. Ely Culbertson wrote:

> A deck of cards was built like the purest of hierarchies, with every card a master to those below it, a lackey to those above it. And there were "masses"— long suits—which always asserted themselves in the end, triumphing over the kings and aces.

Vive la Révolution!

Face cards have historical counterparts upon which they are based:

Jack of Hearts	—La Hire
Jack of Diamonds	—Hector
Jack of Clubs	—Lancelot
Jack of Spades	—Ogier
Queen of Hearts	—Judith
Queen of Diamonds	—Rachel
Queen of Clubs	—Argine
Queen of Spades	—Palas
King of Hearts	—Charlemagne
King of Diamonds	—Caesar
King of Clubs	—Alexander
King of Spades	—David

Imagine Black Bart telling the table he's got a pretty little straight: Charlemagne, Rachel, and Hector.

Card games are often based upon a hierarchical play of besting a card or hand. Remember the joy you felt when you mastered War and Go Fish? I remember it as if it were yesterday —actually it probably was.

Here is an Andy Rooney question for you: Why is it that only the boys seemed to know what hands won when you played strip poker? And why did a flush beat a straight one hand and not the next? So, for the Strip Poker Title of the Universe, keep this on hand, compliments of the Bat Masterson School of Gambling. In descending order:

	Chances of Being Dealt in Five Cards
Royal Flush	1 in 649,740
Straight Flush	1 in 72,193
Four of a Kind	1 in 4,165
Full House	1 in 694
Flush	1 in 509
Straight	1 in 255
Three of a Kind	1 in 47
Two Pair	1 in 21
One Pair	1 in $2\frac{2}{5}$
No Pair	1 in 2

Tournament bridge is the most complicated team game in cards (unless you consider competitive card houses a team sport). These tournaments are easily as emotional and as pressure-filled as Wimbledon, the U.S. Open, or World Cup Soccer. If James Bond played bridge (as I am sure he did) he would have had a long way to go to be as cool as a Life Master.

According to the American Contract Bridge League, players are rated thus:

Sub-Master:	a player who has less than 1 full master point recorded by the League

Junior Master:	a player who has 1 or more master points
Master:	a player who has 20 or more master points
National Master:	a player who has 50 or more master points
Senior Master:	a player who has 100 or more master points
Advanced Senior Master:	a player who has 200 or more master points of which at least 20 must be colored (red or gold) points
Life Master:	a player who has 300 or more master points including at least 50 colored points

The point system is explained in terms of master points:

Rating Points: 100 rating points equal 1 master point
Black Points: Points won at Club Games, Unit Champion-
                 ships, Sectional Tournaments, and various
                 side and special games at Regional and
                 North American Championship tourna-
                 ments
Red Points: Points won in specified Regional, Grand Na-
                 tional, and North American Championship
                 events
Gold Points: Points awarded for section firsts and over-
                 all awards in Regional rated or North
                 American Championship events which have
                 no upper master point restrictions

A serious game requires serious titles and a serious point structure.

Chess is not only one of the most cerebral of games, it is one of the most hierarchical as well. The expression "rank and file" derives from the design of the chess board. The file refers to the frontward and backward movements on the board and the rank refers to the sideways movements.

The actual pieces were given a numerical rank by John Scarne, according to their relative power and importance:

Pawn = 1
Knight = 3
Bishop = 3
Castle (Rook) = 5
Queen = 9

The king is not assigned a number because the object of the game is to capture the board by placing the king in checkmate.

Scarne's ranking of importance is subject to exceptions. Two bishops are usually stronger than a knight and a bishop, and some players are more adept with one than the other. There

was a time in the history of chess when the bishops were valued more highly than knights but modern play has made them equals.

Keep in mind the power of the pieces the next time you lay out a Nimzo-Indian defense.

Go fish.

Popular board games that have withstood the test of time, you will find, are often based upon hierarchical point systems similar to chess or bridge. The idea is to win points, capture opponents, and make it safely to home base.

Ranking in popularity and longevity, along with Parcheesi and Monopoly, is the word game Scrabble. Scrabble is an international favorite, having been translated into dozens of languages. Scrabble players even have their own newsletter about interesting variations, strategies, and competitions.

The letters are carved into tiles and the idea is to form a

crossword puzzle while gathering points. To real Scrabble en-
thusiasts, there are few things in life as satisfying as using
"quetzal"—a South American bird—on a triple word score.

The letters are valued:

0	1	2	3	4	5	6	7	8	9	10
blank	A	D	B	F	K	—	—	J	—	Q
	E	G	C	H				X		Z
	I		M	V						
	L		P	W						
	N			Y						
	O									
	R									
	S									
	T									
	U									

Why there are no letters valued at six, seven, or nine is a
mystery known only to Selchow & Righter Company, which
markets Scrabble.

Some sports are relatively straightforward when it comes to
ranking players and holding tournaments. In tennis, for example, players are "seeded" according to their estimated ability,

their recent win/loss ratio, and their known proficiency.

Other sports have very specific rules about the ranking of players. Judo, for example, is quite rigid about its system of belts and promotions. The promotion system differs from country to country, from school to school, and from teacher to teacher. There is, however, a fundamental consistency to the belt, or sash, awarded to a student of Judo.

An aspiring student works his or her way through the six "kyu" stages and then moves into the actual degrees of "dan," of which there are thirteen. Few have ever attained the final degrees of Judan (10 dan) through Shihan (13 dan). Promotions are based upon an exam wherein one's proficiency, knowledge, moral character, and ability to demonstrate certain techniques are tested.

Rank	U.S.	Europe	Study Time
Rokkyu (6 kyu)	white	white	first day
Gokyu (5 kyu)	white	yellow	4–8 months
Yonkyu (4 kyu)	white	orange	8–12 months
Sankyu (3 kyu)	brown	green	12–18 months
Nikyu (2 kyu)	brown	blue	18–30 months
Ikkyu (1 kyu)	brown	brown	2–4 years
Shodan (1 dan)	black	black	3–5 years
Nidan (2 dan)	black	black	4–6 years
Sandan (3 dan)	black	black	6–11 years
Yodan (4 dan)	black	black	over 9 years
Godan (5 dan)	black	black	over 11 years
Rokudan (6 dan)	black or white	black or white	over 11 years
Shichidan (7 dan)	black or white	black or white	
Hachidan (8 dan)	black or white	black or white	
Kudan (9 dan)	black or red	black or red	

Originally there were only black and white sashes. This was a simple method of keeping the teachers distinguishable from the students.

There have only been approximately twenty-five Kudan ever awarded and there is no way of gauging how long the higher degrees of dan take to achieve.

Similarly, karate sashes were originally colored to differentiate the master from the student. (I think a simple test of skill would clear up any confusion rather speedily.) White symbolized the clean slate of the student who was, as yet, untainted by the sinister knowledge of karate. Black represented the master's total knowledge and complete control. As karate developed, more belts were added to distinguish beginners from the more advanced students.

The present ranking system used in the United States is:

White	novice
Yellow	basic blocks, stances, kicks, and punches
Green	all basic techniques have been mastered
Purple	most intermediate-level techniques have been mastered
Brown	all intermediate-level techniques have been mastered
Black	most of the advanced techniques have been mastered

There are, then, ten degrees to a black belt with ten being the most proficient.

How did these incredibly effective methods of self-defense evolve? The sumptuary laws handed down by the shoguns included special regulations prohibiting the peasants and farmers from owning weapons. Only the illustrious samurai were entitled to carry weapons and to know how to use them. The rabble were left to fend for themselves with what they had on hand.

Colors have long been used as symbols of rank, degree, and prestige. Although not standardized internationally, ski areas, for example, rate the difficulty of their slopes with the following trail markers:

Green Circle	—beginner slopes
Blue Square	—intermediate slopes
Black Diamond	—expert slopes

Learning how to stop yourself when on skis is, naturally, high up on the list of things to learn when first taking to the slopes. Bellowing "Outtamyway, outtacontrol" is considered *de trop* by the Swiss Ski School. The second most important thing to learn is how to read these trail markers. Ask for the name of the slope. Ski resorts cannot resist naming their slopes. Use your common sense when deciding between Bambi's Joy or Buttercup Lane and Thrill Kill or Death Wish.

If you invested in a weekend ski package but could not force

your unwilling legs onto the bunny slope, try cross-country
skiing. When the instructor asks you to rate yourself, use one
of the following terms to show him you know your stuff:

Beginner:	can handle gentle fields and short distances
Novice:	can exert reasonably good control, can do a snowplow turn, and can safely make it down a slight incline
Intermediate:	an experienced skier capable of negotiating most trails and can descend hills of a 20% incline
Expert:	a hardy type who can manage any trail at reasonable speed and can bushwhack through rough terrain. This is also known as 4-wheel drive.

You survived the skiing weekend and it's now July and hot enough to require a weekend in nature. White water canoeing, rafting, or tubing can make you feel like you are truly a member of the Pepsi Generation. Here, then, is the International Scale of Water Difficulty from the American Whitewater Affiliation:

unsuitable for open canoes

Class I:	Moving water with a few riffles and small waves. Few or no obstructions.
Class II:	Easy rapids with waves up to 3 feet and wide, clear channels that are obvious without scouting. Some maneuvering is required.
Class III:	Rapids with high, irregular waves often capable of swamping an open canoe. Narrow passages that often require complex maneuvering. May require some scouting from shore.
Class IV:	Long, difficult rapids with constricted passages that often require precise maneuvering in very turbulent waters. Scouting from shore is necessary, and conditions make rescue difficult. Generally not possible for open canoes. Boaters in covered canoes and kayaks should have the ability to Eskimo roll.
Class V:	Extremely difficult, long, and very violent rapids with highly congested routes, which should always be scouted from shore. Rescue conditions are difficult, and there is significant hazard to life in the event of a mishap. Ability to Eskimo roll is essential for boaters in kayaks and decked canoes.
Class VI:	Difficulties of Class V carried to the extreme of navigability. Nearly impossible and very dangerous. For teams of experts only, after close study has been made and all precautions have been taken.

These grades apply to water above 50°F. If the water is under 50°F and the trip takes you into uncharted wilderness, the river should be considered one class more difficult. Then again, you could always throw your towel and radio into the car and head for the nice, safe pool.

The American Red Cross teaches water safety and lifesaving

if you don't feel as confident in or near the water as you might like to. Anyone who has attended summer camp or has spent time at a YMCA or YWCA probably has a lifesavers' certificate squirreled away somewhere in a desk drawer. The Red Cross rates their courses as:

Beginner Swimmer
Advanced Beginner Swimmer
Intermediate Swimmer
Swimmer
Advanced Swimmer

Once you have passed the Advanced Swimmer course, you may want to consider Basic Rescue, and then, Advanced Life-saving. The rubber duck you save might be your own.

Color delineations are very much in evidence at an archery tournament. The target is coded as follows:

Color	Points
Gold (bull's-eye)	9
Red	7
Blue	5
Black	3
White	1
Petticoat (outside white ring)	0

If the arrow goes through the target, you receive seven points regardless of where it actually entered. If the arrow hits the target but bounces off, you are awarded five points regardless of where it struck the target. If the arrow touches the line between two rings, the higher score is counted.

In an archery tournament the person in charge of the men's team is called the Field Captain and the person in charge of the women's team is called the Lady Paramount. The shooters elect a target captain, a scorer, a drawer (who removes arrows from the target and calls the score), an observer (these archery tournaments must be rather boring if the shooters have to go to these lengths to guarantee a spectator), and an arrow hound. The arrow hound retrieves errant arrows and soothes local farmers while extracting a renegade arrow from a prize Guernsey.

When a golfer yells, *"Bull's-eye!,"* you may assume he or she just managed a hole in one. Sportsfolk have their own language (ask Howard Cosell). Golfers refer to a hole in one as an ace; an eagle is scored when you are two strokes under par; a birdie is one stroke under par. One the other hand, a bogey is one stroke over par, a double bogey is two strokes over, and so on.

England (a golf-mad country) at one time referred to hitting par as a bogey. If you are a P. G. Wodehouse fan, you may remember coming across this term when he got his ball holed in the required number of strokes. This might be a bit confusing unless you are aware of this archaic nomenclature. The British have, if somewhat reluctantly, come around to the American way of golfing and now refer to a par as a par. Strangely, they insist on using their own regulation ball which, for the record, weighs 1.62 ounces. The American whopper weighs in at 1.68 ounces.

There is an age-old argument among golfers as to what the most difficult golf course in the world is. I happen to know it: Pine Valley Golf Club is rumored to be the world's toughest course. Pine Valley is located in Clementon, New Jersey, for you masochists out there.

If you watch any midday television on Sundays, you have to have seen diving (low- and high-board) competitions and wondered how those stony-faced judges arrive at their scores.

It is based on a complicated formula reflecting a variety of factors that the judges take into consideration and that are much too complex to break down. There are some two thousand dives an athlete might attempt, and the judges consider different criteria to arrive at the scores they flip on their boards.

Somersault (rated by half somersaults)
Twist (rated by half twists)
Flight Position: Tuck
                      Pike
                      Straight
                      Free
                      Fly

Position off the Board: Forward
                             Back
                             Reverse
                             Inward

Unnatural Entry (youch!):   Group 1— Forward
                                        Inward
                                        Armstand reverse
                                        (platform)
                               Group 2— Back
                                        Reverse
                                        Armstand forward
                                        (platform)

Approach   Forward
              Back
              Reverse (standing forward, diving back)
              Inward (standing back, diving in)
              Armstand (platform)

   The dives are rated according to their degrees of difficulty, ranging from a low of 1.2 to a high of 3.5. The most easily rated dive is a forward dive in a tuck position off a meter board. The toughest dive is a forward 4½ somersault. You can add two extra points if you are attempting any of these in an above the ground, backyard pool.

Like ski slopes, mountain and rock climbs are rated according to their degrees of difficulty. However, there is no internationally accepted ranking system. Everyone seems to have his own.

The French "Vallot" system is used for alpine climbing in Europe and in England. An adjective is used to give an overall grade to a big route:

PD   Peu Difficile (a bit difficult)
AD   Assez Difficile (fairly difficult)
D   Difficile (difficult)
TD   Très Difficile (very difficult)
ED   Extrêmement Difficile (extremely difficult)

These take into account length, seriousness, and objective dangers on the climb. The hardest individual pitches are then given a numerical classification from I to VI. This rates technical difficulty under normal conditions. Some climbers have introduced a VII rating. Artificial (aid) pitches are graded A1 through A4.

The British use three domestic systems with the traditional delineations:

M   Moderate
D   Difficult
VD   Very Difficult
S   Severe
VS   Very Severe
ES   Extremely Severe

There are subdivisions of "easy," "mild," and "hard," and a numerical system I through VI (with a, b, and c subdivisions) reserved for especially difficult outcrops.

In the United States we use the California Decimal System:

Class 3:   easy ground "scrambling"—no need for a rope
Class 4:   may need a rope
Class 5:   rope and protection needed. This class is subdivided into 5.1 through 5.10 rating, 5.10 being the most difficult.

Does all this sound unnecessarily complicated? Rock climb in Australia then. The Aussies have a totally arbitrary system rated 1 through 21. I gather that if a particular climb strikes someone as more difficult than the last 21-rated climb, a 22nd rating will be added.

Boxers fight according to their body weight and win/loss record. Rocky just lucked out when he was given a chance to duke it out with the heavyweight champ of the world.

Most fans of boxing follow the heavyweights because, well, they are the heavyweights and like Sly Stallone they get the press, the prestige, the beer commercials, and the big bucks.

Some boxers fight in different weight divisions as they put on and take off pounds.

Division	*Weight in Pounds*
Heavyweight	over 175
Light Heavyweight	no more than 175
Middleweight	no more than 160

Welterweight	no more than 148
Lightweight	no more than 135
Featherweight	no more than 126
Bantamweight	no more than 118
Flyweight	no more than 112

The Junior Division is a bit less complicated:

Lightweight	no more than 130
Welterweight	no more than 140
Middleweight	no more than 154

Winning guarantees you the spot atop the pyramid. Gold (symbol of wealth, rarity and endurance) is fashioned into a medal. Blue (symbol of royalty, strength and stature) is the color of victory. Champagne (excellence, quality and snob appeal) is customarily poured over the winner's head.

From musical chairs to the Olympic Games, the idea is to defeat the opposition, beat the clock, and conquer the odds, thereby moving up the ladder to the summit. Games and sports are hierarchies in motion.

Conclusion

It should be obvious now that we are creatures crazy for hierarchies. We are destined to assign everything a place, a pigeonhole, a niche.

Our language and expressions reflect our predilection toward hierarchical thinking. "Chef" is French for chief. "Premier" is another French word meaning "first." Top dog, kingpin, top brass and overlord lord over the low man on the totem pole, flunky, and underling.

We may be created equal but we don't stay that way for long.

> The heavens themselves, the planets, and this center,
> Observe degree, priority and place,
> Insisture, course, proportion, season, form,
> Office and custom, in all line of order.
> —*Troilus and Cressida*, I, III
> William Shakespeare

FINIS.